Intoxicated CUPCAKES

41 TIPSY TREATS

Kate Legere

RUNNING PRESS
PHILADELPHIA · LONDON

Published by Running Press, a Member of the Perseus
Books Group

Books published by Running Press are available at
special discounts for bulk purchases in the United States by
corporations, institutions, and other organizations. For
more information, please contact the Special
Markets Department at the Perseus Books Group,
2300 Chestnut Street, Suite 200, Philadelphia,
PA 19103, or call (800) 810-4145, ext. 5000, or e-mail
special.markets@perseusbooks.com.

ISBN 978-0-7624-3873-0
Library of Congress Control Number: 2010940970

E-book ISBN 978-0-7624-4364-2

9 8 7 6 5 4 3 2
Digit on the right indicates the number of this printing

Edited by Jordana Tusman
Cover and interior design by Jason Kayser
Food styling by Katrina Tekavec
Typography: Adobe Caslon, Cenizas, and Verlag

The publisher would like to thank the following
retailers for their invaluable assistance in the
production of this book: Simon Pierce in West Chester,
PA, and Sur La Table and Crate and Barrel in King
of Prussia, PA.

Running Press Book Publishers
2300 Chestnut Street
Philadelphia, PA 19103-4371

Visit us on the web!
www.runningpress.com

This book is dedicated to my mom, whose
enthusiasm, encouragement, belief in the idea, and
two a.m. photo shoots made it all possible.

Contents

Acknowledgments 9

Introduction 10

Baking Tips and Tricks 13

Sweet Stuff 19

BANANA UPSIDE-DOWN CUPCAKES, 21

BUTTERY CINNAMONY CUPCAKES, 22

COCOA COLADA CUPCAKES, 24

PIÑA COLADA CUPCAKES, 27

DESIGNATED DRIVER CUPCAKES, 29

"EVERYTHING'S GONNA BE ALL WHITE"
CHOCOLATE CUPCAKES, 30

LIMONCELLO POPPY SEED CUPCAKES, 33

GRAMMY LOVES POP-POP
CUPCAKES, 34

HOT TODDY CUPCAKES, 36

MANGO MARGARITA CUPCAKES, 39

STRAWBERRY DAIQUIRI CUPCAKES, 40

TOP O' THE MORNING CUPCAKES, 42

WHITE CHOCOLATE AND RASPBERRY
CUPCAKES, 44

Fun Stuff 47

BLOODY MARY CUPCAKES, 49

BRIGHT AND CHEERY ORANGE
RASPBERRY CUPCAKES, 50

CAR BOMB CUPCAKES, 53

DARK AND STORMY CUPCAKES, 57

SPIKED EGGNOG CUPCAKES, 58

MINTY MOJITO CUPCAKES, 60

TOOTY-FRUITY SANGRIA CUPCAKES, 63

NOT YOUR GRANNY'S APPLE CUPCAKES, 64

RUM AND CARROT CUPCAKES, 67

Fancy Stuff 71

BELGIAN BEAUTY CUPCAKES, 73

BELLINI BELLE CUPCAKES, 75

CHAMPAGNE PARTY CUPCAKES, 77

CHOCOLATE GRAND MARNIER® CUPCAKES, 79

FANCY PANTS GOLDEN GINGERBREAD
CUPCAKES, 81

NAKED GEISHA CUPCAKES, 83

FIERY RED VELVET CUPCAKES, 84

OH-SO-DECADENT PEAR AND
HAZELNUT CUPCAKES, 86

WINE AND CHEESE PARTY CUPCAKES, 89

Hard Stuff 93

A BIT O' SOUTHERN PRIDE CUPCAKES, 94

BOURBON BALL SURPRISE
CUPCAKES, 97

COSMO CUPCAKES, 100

DARK STOUT CHOCOLATE
CUPCAKES, 102

TEQUILA SUNRISE CUPCAKES, 105

JÄGER® BOMB CUPCAKES, 108

RUM AND COLA CUPCAKES, 111

Fast and Easy Stuff 113

FUZZY NAVEL CUPCAKES, 114

MINT GRASSHOPPER CUPCAKES, 117

MUDSLIDE CUPCAKES, 118

DIY Cupcake Stencils 120

DIY Cupcake Wrappers 122

Index 125

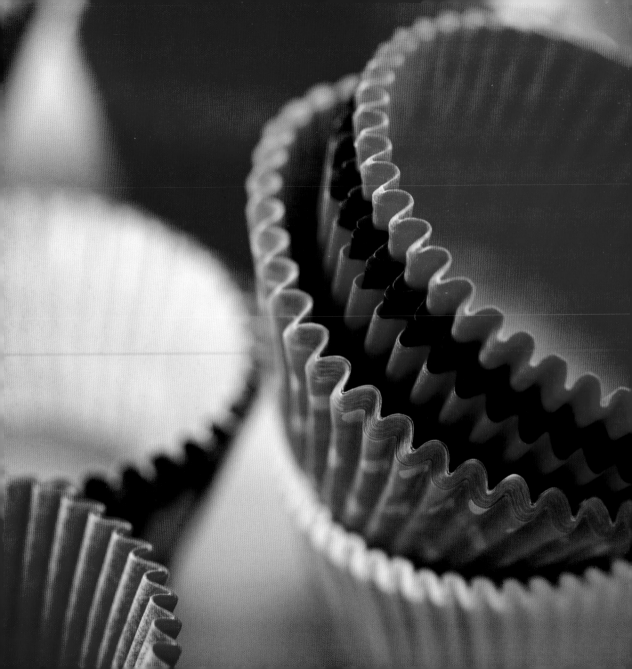

Acknowledgments

This book would not be possible without the help from all of my friends and family who left me with half-empty bottles and who graciously ate endless cupcakes in the name of research: especially Mom, Dad, Meggie-o, Marc, Sonya, Gram, Pop, Brian, and Stacy. Thanks to Mimi for all the cupcake research and the aunts and uncles who were there when it all started: Uncle Art, Bob, T, and Tom; and Aunt Barbara, Elva, Mary Jane, and Paula.

I have amazing friends who helped by baking and baking and baking to help perfect the recipes. Your feedback made the book what it is today. Thank you to Alisa, Amanda, Antonya, Barbara, Claire, Garth, Gloria, Janice, Jenna, Joshua, Kathy, Kimbo, Kristen, Kylie, Maria, Marian, Martha, Mary Jane, Matt, Meg, Melinda, Michelle, Mom, Paula, Sonya, Stacy, Sugi, and Suzanne.

Thank you to my editor, Jordana Tusman, who shared my enthusiasm and vision for *Intoxicated Cupcakes* from the first time we spoke.

A special thanks to my special sweet, Kevster, who had his hand on my back the whole time.

Introduction

*"Nothing would be more tiresome than
eating and drinking if God had not made them
a pleasure as well as a necessity."*

—VOLTAIRE

You threw a fabulous party. You created the perfect playlist. Everyone danced. You finally tried those adorable little appetizers from the magazines and they turned out even better than expected. And, as only the hostess with the mostest could, you pulled off some super-fancy mixed drinks. Good for you!

But, that was last night. Today, there are empty glasses all over the house. (And who left without their shoes?) Now you have all these half-finished bottles of booze left over and, well, what's a girl to do? Start with a little "hair of the dog that bit you," but then what? *Intoxicated Cupcakes* offers just the thing. Here, two vices that have gotten us all through some

rough patches come together in this sexy little cookbook. Cupcakes and booze: has there ever been a more perfect combination?

If you're going to a wine and cheese party, why not whip up the Wine and Cheese Party Cupcakes? If you're going to a Mexican-themed party, how about Tequila Sunrise Cupcakes? A bachelorette party? Champagne Party Cupcakes will do the trick. There is a recipe here for pretty much every occasion, and all of these cupcakes have a special twist that will have your guests begging for more.

I can't tell you how much fun I had putting this cookbook together. Like most ideas, this cookbook was an accident born of necessity.

There I was, enjoying the large kitchen at the rental house, baking the summer away. I was working on a chocolate cake that needed a little oomph, so I ran to the store in search of some mint extract. Two mint-less stores later and I resigned myself to baking a run-of-the mill chocolate cake. One last shot (pun intended) at stepping it up, I looked in the pantry, and . . . voilà! There I saw a bottle of crème de menthe. Of course! From there, the experiments began. Like a lot of folks, I seemed to have amassed quite a stash of half-empty bottles of booze. *Hmmm . . . I wonder what would happen if I used this leftover rum in a carrot cake . . . I wonder if this bit of brandy could intensify an apple cake. . . .* It all just seemed too obvious! Just think, if the supermarket at the Jersey shore had stocked mint extract, you might not be holding this book in your hand and I might never have known that tequila and cake batter make for good bedfellows!

Thanks to my incredible friends and family, I had an eager group of guinea pigs waiting to test out these delicious experiments. I no longer saw parties as simply an excuse to let my hair down and don my dancing shoes; no, these soirées were now ripe opportunities for some market research. Parties became an ideal platform to test my concoctions and no brunch was complete without my Bloody Mary Cupcakes. My little sister's graduation party served as the perfect opportunity to gauge the opinions of the post-college crowd. Unsurprisingly, they wanted more booze!

The kitchen is no longer a place for grannies in knee-high stockings. *Intoxicated Cupcakes* is for the modern baker—in fishnets and high heels! If you love to create and think a little booze can make something sweet even better, this is *the* book for you. I hope you have as much fun with these recipes as I did. So, blast your favorite tunes, throw on a cute little apron, and enjoy *Intoxicated Cupcakes*. And don't forget the importance of sampling a shot or two as you bake!

Love, Kate

BAKING TIPS AND TRICKS

———✦———

I KNOW, I KNOW. LIVING LIFE IN THE MOMENT IS FULFILLING AND all that jazz. With baking, though, it pays to think ahead a bit. Review the tips and tricks below to ensure that your baby beauties will be nothing short of perfection.

When you choose a recipe, always make sure that you have enough of each ingredient before you start baking. Remember, baking is a science, and once those ingredients start reacting, you can't just ask them to take a break while you run off to the store for more baking soda.

If there's a recipe that sounds particularly delicious but you don't have the necessary booze, there's no need to buy a full bottle. Just head to the liquor store and pick up those mini bottles that you can get on airplanes. They're usually hanging out by the front registers.

When measuring ingredients, always use the right tools. Glass measuring cups are for liquid ingredients and nested measuring cups are for dry ingredients. Level your dry ingredients (without packing them down) using the flat edge of a butter knife.

If you're in a rush, do not—I repeat DO NOT—try to soften your butter in the microwave. You want the butter to be solid, not liquid, so that air can get in it as it's beaten. If you are in a rush, just chop it into little bits and you should be ready to go in ten minutes.

Some of the recipes in this book call for a double boiler. A double boiler is used to cook heat-sensitive ingredients slowly and evenly. You can go out and buy a fancy one or make your own. To do this, you will need two pots of different sizes. The smaller should be able to perch on the edges of the larger one (a glass bowl inside a pan is a popular combination). Inside the larger pot you will need to bring 1 to 2 cups of water to a simmer. The steam from this water will heat your top pot, so be sure there's a bit of space in between the water and the top pot. It's as easy as, well, cupcakes!

There are tons of varieties of flour. The main difference often comes down to how much gluten the flour produces when heat and liquid are added into the equation. The less gluten you have, the more tender your product. If your cake is too tender, it will fall apart. If it has too much gluten, it will be tough. The recipes in this cookbook call for either all-purpose flour (more gluten) or cake flour (softer flour with less gluten). If a recipe calls for 1 cup all-purpose flour and you only have cake flour, use 1 cup plus 2 tablespoons cake flour. If a recipe calls for cake flour and you only have all-purpose flour, substitute 1 cup minus 2 tablespoons sifted all-purpose flour.

Food coloring can be a baker's best friend, but if you don't use enough you'll have a washed-out-looking cupcake (or icing) and too much will leave your baked goods looking like some crazy hippie flashback. Food coloring comes in different levels of concentration. The recipes contained in this cookbook offer suggested food coloring amounts, but you should use your own baker's discretion based on the concentration of your chosen food coloring and until you reach the desired color. Personally, I love the food coloring gels that are found at baking specialty stores and some craft shops. These gels are a bit more expensive than

the liquid drops from the grocery store, but you have a full rainbow of colors to choose from and you only need to use about one-third the amount of food coloring gels than you would the drops.

Cupcake liners should be filled between ⅔ to ¾ of the way with batter. Follow the suggested yield for each recipe and you will bake beautiful, perfect-sized cupcakes.

A crowded house party makes for a good time. A crowded oven makes for uneven baking. Give those babies some room to breathe and never let your pans touch the sides of the oven.

After washing your cupcake pan, put it in your oven as it's cooling down. The heat will eliminate the moisture and will keep your pan from rusting.

Going somewhere? Your local grocery store's bakery department probably has some donut boxes to spare. Ask someone at the counter if you can take an empty box. I've never been told *no*. Of course you could always go out and buy a cupcake carrier, but you have to deal with that whole remembering-your-cupcake-carrier-at-the-end-of-the-night thing.

We eat with our eyes before we eat with our mouths. If your food doesn't look appetizing, it won't *taste* appetizing. You are a pastry artist, so look at your cupcake as a blank canvas. Carefully smoothing the icing onto your cupcake is one way to do it. You can also get pretty cheap pastry tips at your local craft or kitchen store. Have fun experimenting with different tips. Of course, a simple ziplock bag with a hole (½ inch in diameter) cut in one corner will also do the trick. Fill the bag with icing and squeeze it out of the corner in a circular motion, working from the outside of the cupcake inward.

Each recipe indicates whether you should wait for the cupcakes to cool before icing them. Consider this your zen time and don't rush it. Unless a recipe specifically calls for applying the topping while the cupcakes are still warm, wait it out. Otherwise, your warm cupcakes will melt your icing and render them a frothy flat mess. It's not a good look for a cupcake!

Cupcakes store best when unfrosted. Keep unfrosted cupcakes in an airtight container with a slice of bread. The bread will absorb the moisture and keep the cupcakes from going soggy. You can keep your icing in the fridge and rewhip it before applying. You can also freeze your cupcakes and icing separately, defrost them both, and assemble them as needed.

Cupcakes that are already frosted should keep well for two to three days, unless otherwise indicated in the recipe. If the cupcake has whipped cream topping or cream cheese icing, store it in the refrigerator. Unfrosted frozen cupcakes should keep for up to three months.

A few must-haves for cupcake bakers:

+ A good rubber spatula! It's worth the small investment. The better the spatula, the less batter wasted.

+ Ice cream scoopers! Use one to evenly divide your batter among the cups. Brilliant!

+ Shiny pans! Who doesn't like shiny things? Especially when they reflect the heat, thereby slowing the baking process, which will help your precious cupcakes from getting over-cooked on the edges and undercooked on the inside.

+ An oven thermometer! Until you know your oven intimately, use an oven thermometer to ensure proper baking times and temperatures.

+ A flour sifter! To ensure clump-free flour, baking soda, and other dry ingredients, your sifter is your best friend. You can use a proper sifter if you prefer, but just a plain old mesh strainer will do just fine.

All right, enough! It's time to get down to business and create some deliciously booze-infused cupcakes.

SWEET STUFF

---◆∞◆---

SOME DRINKS JUST AREN'T MEANT FOR MEN. LUCKILY, US GIRLS can pretty much drink anything: beers with the boys when the game is on and umbrella-adorned cocktails with our lady friends. These recipes are dedicated to the fruity drinks that men secretly like, but are always too afraid to order. Drinks served in oversized glasses; drinks decked out with frilly accoutrements; drinks that taste like a sunny summer day; and drinks that taste like Christmas—that special time of year when calories can go to hell! But just because it's sweet, doesn't mean it's bad for you. Delve into Sweet Stuff and you'll find the cold-curing Hot Toddy Cupcakes, the fruit-filled Mango Margarita Cupcakes, or the Designated Driver Cupcakes for the good girl. And the best thing about these recipes is that most of us have several bottles of these sweet liqueurs left over from our last girl's night. And if you don't, well, it gives you a good excuse to refill that lucky liquor cabinet!

Banana Upside-Down Cupcakes

THESE CUPCAKES SMELL ABSOLUTELY DIVINE AS THEY BAKE and they taste just as great when you bite into them. Serve them warm with a scoop of vanilla ice cream and your taste buds won't know how to thank you.

1. Preheat the oven to 350°F. Lightly grease each cup in a 12-cup cupcake pan. Set aside.

2. For the topping, melt the butter in a small saucepan. Stir in the sugar and cinnamon until blended. Remove from the heat and add the chopped bananas. Spoon about 2 tablespoons of the topping into each cup in the pan.

3. In a clean bowl, beat the egg white until stiff peaks form. Set aside.

4. In a large bowl, beat the butter and sugar with an electric mixer until fluffy. Beat in the egg yolk and vanilla.

5. In a small bowl, combine the flour, baking powder, and salt. Alternate between adding the flour mixture and the banana liqueur to the batter, beating well after each addition.

6. Gently fold the beaten egg white into the batter.

7. Pour the batter evenly into the cupcake pan. Bake at 350°F for 20 to 25 minutes, or until a toothpick inserted into the center of the cupcake comes out clean. Cool the pan on a wire rack for 10 minutes. Invert the pan over a cookie sheet and gently tap the bottom of each cup to release the cupcakes. Serve them warm with vanilla ice cream.

Makes 12

FOR THE BANANA TOPPING:

4 tablespoons salted butter

7 tablespoons dark brown sugar, packed

1 teaspoon ground cinnamon

2 ripe bananas, cut into 2-inch-long sticks

FOR THE CUPCAKES:

1 large egg, at room temperature, separated

4 tablespoons unsalted butter, at room temperature

¼ cup granulated sugar

1 teaspoon vanilla extract

1 cup cake flour

1½ teaspoons baking powder

¼ teaspoon salt

½ cup banana liqueur

Buttery Cinnamony Cupcakes

Makes 24

FOR THE CUPCAKES:

2 cups all-purpose flour

1 tablespoon baking powder

2 teaspoons ground cinnamon

¾ teaspoon salt

⅔ cup butter-flavored shortening

1¼ cups granulated sugar

1 teaspoon vanilla extract

3 large eggs

⅓ cup whole milk

⅓ cup butterscotch schnapps

FOR THE ICING:

2 (8-ounce) packages cream cheese, at room temperature

4 ounces (1 stick) unsalted butter, at room temperature

2 cups confectioners' sugar, sifted

1 teaspoon ground cinnamon

2 teaspoons butterscotch schnapps

24 cinnamon-flavored gummy candies, for topping

THERE'S SOMETHING QUITE COMFORTING ABOUT THE TASTE of cinnamon and butter mixed together. You'll know exactly what I mean when you smell these bad boys baking in the oven. It'll take you back to a simpler time in your life . . . but with a little bit of booze!

1. Preheat the oven to 350°F. Line a cupcake pan with 24 cupcake liners. Set aside.

2. In a small bowl, sift together the flour, baking powder, cinnamon, and salt.

3. In a large bowl, use an electric mixer to beat together the shortening, sugar, and vanilla until light and fluffy. Add the eggs, one at a time, beating well after each addition.

4. In a second small bowl, mix together the milk and schnapps. Alternate between adding the milk mixture and the flour mixture into the shortening mixture.

5. Pour the batter into the prepared cups. Bake for 18 to 22 minutes, or until a toothpick inserted into the center of the cupcake comes out clean. Cool on a wire rack for 5 minutes, or until cool enough to handle. Remove the cupcakes from the pan and cool completely.

6. For the icing, use an electric mixer to beat the cream cheese and butter until well mixed. Slowly add the sugar, cinnamon, and schnapps and beat on medium-high until smooth and fluffy. Smooth the icing onto the cooled cupcakes and garnish with a cinnamon candy.

KATE'S TIP: Don't forget: the special ingredient is the cinnamon. And you don't have to stop with the cinnamon in the cupcake. Go ahead and grate some fresh cinnamon atop the icing.

Cocoa Colada Cupcakes

FOR THE CUPCAKES:

2 cups all-purpose flour

1¾ cups granulated sugar

¾ cup cocoa powder

½ teaspoon salt

1 tablespoon baking soda

1 large egg

⅔ cup vegetable oil

¾ cup buttermilk

¼ cup Irish cream liqueur

1 cup crushed canned pineapple, drained

½ cup coconut rum

FOR THE CHOCOLATE GLAZE:

1½ cups semisweet chocolate chips

6 tablespoons unsalted butter

2 tablespoons light corn syrup

2 tablespoons coconut rum

½ cup shredded coconut, for topping

FRESH OUT OF COLLEGE, I STUMBLED ACROSS A WELL-PAYING job as a liquor promoter, giving out free samples at grocery stores on Sunday mornings. These cupcakes are based on one of my favorite drinks that I used to give to early morning shoppers. The subtle flavor combination of choco-late, pineapple, and coconut makes for a delicious drink and an even tastier cupcake.

1. Preheat the oven to 350°F. Line a cupcake pan with 24 cupcake liners. Set aside.

2. In a medium bowl, sift together the flour, sugar, cocoa powder, salt, and baking soda. Set aside.

3. In a large bowl, use an electric mixer on medium speed to beat together the egg, oil, buttermilk, Irish cream liqueur, pineapple, and rum until well combined. Turn the mixer to low and add the flour mixture, beating just until combined.

4. Divide the batter evenly among the cupcake liners and bake for 16 to 20 minutes, or until a toothpick inserted into the center of the cupcake comes out clean. Cool on a wire rack for 5 minutes, or until cool enough to handle. Remove the cupcakes from the pan and cool completely.

5. For the glaze, heat the chocolate chips, butter, and corn syrup atop a double boiler (see page 14) set at low heat. Stir continuously until the chocolate melts, and then remove from the heat. Add the rum and stir until smooth. Drizzle the glaze atop the cooled cupcakes and add a touch of shredded coconut to each.

> **KATE'S TIP:** A candied pineapple chunk would look divine popping out of the icing. And if you're feeling like **REALLY** going over the top, you could go a step farther and dip the pineapple in melted chocolate!

Piña Colada Cupcakes

WHO CARES WHETHER IT'S SUMMER OR NOT? THESE TROPICAL cupcakes are refreshing, light, and full of flavor. Close your eyes and you can almost feel the sand between your toes!

1. Preheat the oven to 350°F. Line a cupcake pan with 16 cupcake liners. Set aside.

2. In a small bowl, combine the flour and baking powder. Set aside.

3. In a large bowl, use an electric mixer on low speed and beat together the sugar, butter, eggs, vanilla, milk, and rum for 5 minutes, creating a smooth consistency. Add the flour mixture, beating just until combined.

4. Stir in the coconut and pineapple by hand.

5. Pour the batter into the prepared cups. Bake for 20 to 24 minutes, or until a toothpick inserted into the center of the cupcake comes out clean. Cool on a wire rack for 5 minutes, or until cool enough to handle. Remove the cupcakes from the pan and cool completely.

(continued)

Makes 16

FOR THE CUPCAKES:

1½ cups all-purpose flour

½ teaspoon baking powder

1¼ cups granulated sugar

4 ounces (1 stick) plus
2 tablespoons salted butter,
at room temperature

3 large eggs

½ teaspoon vanilla extract

3 tablespoons whole milk

¼ cup coconut rum

¼ cup shredded coconut

½ cup canned pineapple,
chopped and drained

FOR THE ICING:

1½ cups confectioners'
sugar, sifted

6 ounces (1½ sticks) unsalted
butter, at room temperature

3 tablespoons coconut milk

⅓ cup shredded coconut,
for topping

6. For the icing, use an electric mixer on medium-high speed to mix the sugar, butter, and coconut milk until smooth and fluffy. Pipe the frosting onto the cupcakes and decorate with the shredded coconut.

KATE'S TIP: For a colorful alternative to the shredded coconut topping, use yellow sugar crystals. Can't decide between them? Why not use both?!

Designated Driver Cupcakes

EVEN THE BADDEST OF BAD GIRLS NEED TO BE RESPONSIBLE now and again. While your friends are pounding away the six-packs, you can do some pounding of your own with these breath-defying and pound cake–inspired cupcakes. As the name suggests, you can eat the whole batch and drive your girlfriends home at the end of the night.

Makes 12

4 ounces (1 stick) unsalted butter, at room temperature

¼ cup shortening

1 cup granulated sugar

2 large eggs

3 tablespoons grenadine

1 teaspoon vanilla extract

1 teaspoon lemon extract

½ cup lemon-lime soda

1½ cups all-purpose flour

2 tablespoons confectioners' sugar, for dusting

1. Preheat the oven to 325°F. Line a cupcake pan with 12 cupcake liners. Set aside.

2. In a large bowl, use an electric mixer on medium-high speed to beat together the butter, shortening, and sugar until light and fluffy. Add the eggs, one at a time, beating well after each addition. Add the grenadine, vanilla and lemon extracts, and soda, scraping the sides of the bowl as necessary. Turn the mixer to low and add the flour. Beat just until well combined.

3. Divide the batter evenly among the cupcake liners and bake for 16 to 20 minutes, or until a toothpick inserted into the center of the cupcake comes out clean. Cool on a wire rack for 5 minutes, or until cool enough to handle. Remove the cupcakes from the pan and cool completely.

4. Dust the cupcakes with confectioners' sugar.

"Everything's Gonna Be All White" Chocolate Cupcakes

Makes 24

FOR THE CUPCAKES:

2 cups all-purpose flour

3½ teaspoons baking powder

¼ teaspoon salt

1 cup granulated sugar

4 large eggs

8 ounces (2 sticks) salted butter, at room temperature

½ cup white chocolate liqueur

½ cup white chocolate chips

FOR THE FILLING:

1 (1.4-ounce) package instant vanilla pudding mix

½ cup white chocolate liqueur

FOR THE ICING:

1½ cups white chocolate chips

4 ounces (1 stick) unsalted butter, at room temperature

1 tablespoon white chocolate liqueur, warm

⅔ cup white chocolate shavings, for garnish

EXPRESS YOUR PURE AND VIRGINAL SIDE WITH THESE DELICATE white on white cupcakes. But don't be fooled into thinking they are without their little secrets. A dollop of white chocolate pudding awaits your hungry friends when they sink their teeth into the center. Nibble with care.

1. Preheat the oven to 350°F. Line a cupcake pan with 24 cupcake liners. Set aside.

2. In a medium bowl, combine the flour, baking powder, salt, and sugar. Set aside.

3. Combine the eggs, butter, liqueur, and chocolate chips in a large bowl. Use an electric mixer on medium speed to mix the ingredients for 2 to 3 minutes, or until light and creamy. Turn the mixer to medium-low speed and add the flour mixture, blending just until combined.

4. Divide the batter evenly among the cupcake liners and bake for 16 to 20 minutes, or until a toothpick inserted into the center of the cupcake comes out clean. Cool on a wire rack for 5 minutes, or until cool enough to handle. Remove the cupcakes from the pan and cool completely.

(continued)

5. For the filling, combine the pudding mix with the white chocolate liqueur in a small bowl. Whisk for 2 minutes and place in the refrigerator to set for 5 minutes.

6. While the pudding is setting, cut a small hole in the top of each cooled cupcake. Use a piping bag or a sandwich bag with a hole cut in the corner to fill each cupcake hole with pudding. The hole should go about two-thirds of the way down the cupcake.

7. For the icing, heat the chocolate chips in a double boiler (see page 14), at a low temperature. Stir until three-quarters of the chocolate is melted. Remove from the heat and allow the chocolate to cool completely, while stirring.

8. In a bowl, use an electric mixer to beat the butter until light and fluffy. Add the warm white chocolate liqueur. Gradually beat in the cooled chocolate, beating until thick and creamy. Dollop the icing onto the cupcakes and top with the white chocolate shavings.

KATE'S TIP: If you are following a cupcake recipe that calls for you to cut a hole in the top of the cupcake, save your scraps for a little parfait for later. Two desserts in one!

Limoncello Poppy Seed Cupcakes

I CAN'T THINK OF LIMONCELLO WITHOUT REMEMBERING Danny DeVito's hilariously drunken interview on morning TV. (If you've never seen it, look it up on the Internet.) I think it was that interview that brought the traditional Italian liqueur to American mainstream drinkers. It's sweet, lemony, never sour, and adds a fabulous new twist to your traditional poppy seed cupcake.

1. Preheat the oven to 350°F. Line a cupcake pan with 12 cupcake liners. Set aside.

2. In a medium bowl, sift together the flour, baking powder, and salt. Set aside.

3. In a large bowl, use an electric mixer on medium speed to cream together the butter and sugar until light and fluffy. Add the lemon zest until combined. Add the eggs, one at a time, beating until light and fluffy. Add the limoncello and buttermilk until well combined, scraping the bowl as needed. Turn the mixer to low speed and gradually add the poppy seeds and flour mixture, mixing just until combined.

4. Divide the batter evenly among the cupcake liners and bake for 16 to 20 minutes, or until a toothpick inserted into the center of the cupcake comes out clean. Cool on a wire rack for 5 minutes, or until cool enough to handle. Remove the cupcakes from the pan and cool completely.

5. For the glaze, use a fork to mix the sugar and limoncello in a small bowl until smooth. Drizzle the glaze onto the cooled cupcakes.

Makes 12

FOR THE CUPCAKES:

2 cups all-purpose flour

2 teaspoons baking powder

¼ teaspoon salt

4 ounces (1 stick) unsalted butter, at room temperature

⅔ cup granulated sugar

1 teaspoon lemon zest

2 large eggs

½ cup limoncello

½ cup buttermilk

4 teaspoons poppy seeds

FOR THE GLAZE:

1 cup confectioners' sugar, sifted

3 tablespoons limoncello

Grammy Loves Pop-Pop Cupcakes

Makes 18

FOR THE CHOCOLATE-COVERED CHERRIES:

18 maraschino cherries

2¾ teaspoons unsalted butter, at room temperature

1 tablespoon light corn syrup

1½ teaspoons almond liqueur

½ cup confectioners' sugar, sifted

¾ cup semisweet chocolate

FOR THE CUPCAKES:

2¼ cups all-purpose flour

1½ cups granulated sugar

½ cup cocoa powder

1½ teaspoons baking soda

1 teaspoon salt

¾ cup vegetable oil

1 tablespoon vanilla extract

1½ cups strong coffee, at room temperature

¼ cup cherry schnapps

2 tablespoons cider vinegar

THESE CUPCAKES ARE DEDICATED TO THE LOVE SHARED between my grandparents for sixty-seven years. My grammy swears that nobody ever loved another person like she loved Pop-Pop. As a small gesture of love, she would give him a box of chocolate-covered cherries every Valentine's Day, so it's fitting that these cupcakes have a chocolate-covered cherry on the inside. They're certain to put a smile on the face of whomever you give them to.

1. Begin by making the chocolate-covered cherries. Allow the cherries to dry on a paper towel as you make the coating.

2. In a small bowl, combine the butter, corn syrup, and almond liqueur and mix until smooth. Add the sugar and stir to create a thick paste.

3. Wrap each cherry in a thin layer of this paste and chill in the fridge for 10 minutes.

4. Heat the semisweet chocolate in a double boiler (see page 14) at low heat, stirring until three-quarters of the chocolate has melted. Remove from the heat and continue stirring until smooth. Dip each paste-covered cherry in the chocolate and set on parchment paper to cool.

5. Preheat the oven to 350°F. Line a cupcake pan with 18 cupcake liners. Set aside.

6. For the cupcakes, sift together the flour, sugar, cocoa powder, baking soda, and salt in a large bowl. With the electric mixer on low, slowly add the oil and vanilla until fully incorporated.

7. Gradually add the coffee and cherry schnapps. The mixture will separate and then come back together to form a smooth consistency. Add the vinegar, mixing just until combined.

8. Divide the batter evenly among the cupcake liners, filling each cup halfway. Place one chocolate-covered cherry on top of the batter in each cup. Fill with the remaining batter.

9. Bake for 16 to 20 minutes, or until a toothpick inserted into the center of the cupcake comes out clean. Cool on a wire rack for 5 minutes, or until cool enough to handle. Remove the cupcakes from the pan and cool completely.

10. For the icing, beat the butter until light and fluffy. Slowly add the sugar, cocoa powder, and cherry schnapps. Use the electric mixer to beat on medium-high until smooth and fluffy. Smooth the icing onto the cooled cupcakes.

FOR THE ICING:

4 ounces (1 stick) salted butter, at room temperature

2 cups confectioners' sugar, sifted

¼ cup cocoa powder

¼ cup cherry schnapps

Hot Toddy Cupcakes

Makes 16

FOR THE CUPCAKES:

2 cups all-purpose flour

1½ cups granulated sugar

½ teaspoon salt

1 tablespoon baking powder

½ cup whole milk

½ cup Long Island iced tea mix (with alcohol)

½ cup vegetable oil

3 large eggs, beaten

1 tablespoon grated orange zest

FOR THE ICING:

1 (8-ounce) package cream cheese, at room temperature

1½ cups confectioners' sugar, sifted

⅓ cup honey

3 to 6 drops orange food coloring

Silver embellishment candies or citrus candy fruit slices, for garnish

FEELING A LITTLE UNDER THE WEATHER? GO EASY ON YOURSELF, stay inside today, and keep your jammies on. Treat yourself to a good old movie and bake these comforting cupcakes. The honey icing is just heavenly and is sure to be just the cold-curing trick you need to get you back on your feet.

1. Preheat the oven to 350°F. Line a cupcake pan with 16 cupcake liners. Set aside.

2. In a medium bowl, sift together the flour, sugar, salt, and baking powder. Set aside.

3. In a large bowl, combine the milk, iced tea mix, oil, eggs, and orange zest. With the electric mixer on low speed, slowly add the flour mixture and blend just until combined.

4. Pour the batter into the prepared cups. Bake for 16 to 20 minutes, or until a toothpick inserted into the center of the cupcake comes out clean. Cool on a wire rack for 5 minutes, or until cool enough to handle. Remove the cupcakes from the pan and cool completely.

5. For the icing, beat together the cream cheese and sugar until light and creamy. With the mixer on medium, add the honey and enough food coloring until the mixture is a pale orange.

6. Spoon the icing onto the cooled cupcakes and decorate with edible silver embellishments or citrus candy fruit slices.

Mango Margarita Cupcakes

HOW DO YOU MAKE AN ALREADY TROPICAL DRINK EVEN MORE tropical? Add a bit of mango, of course! These fruit-filled delights are moist and full of surprises.

1. Preheat the oven to 350°F. Line a cupcake pan with 20 cupcake liners. Set aside.

2. In a medium bowl, sift together the flour, salt, sugar, and baking powder. Set aside.

3. In a large bowl, combine the milk, margarita mix, tequila, oil, eggs, lime zest, and mango. With the electric mixer on low speed, slowly add the flour mixture and blend just until combined.

4. Pour the batter into the prepared cups. Bake for 16 to 20 minutes, or until a toothpick inserted into the center of the cupcake comes out clean. Cool on a wire rack for 5 minutes, or until cool enough to handle. Remove the cupcakes from the pan and cool completely.

5. For the icing, use a fork to mix the sugar and lime juice. Once smooth, drizzle onto the cooled cupcakes. Top with the mango pieces and sugar crystals.

> **KATE'S TIP:** Want to add the dried mango pieces to the icing? After you've mixed the sugar and lime juice until smooth, go ahead and add some dried mango to it.

Makes 20

FOR THE CUPCAKES:

2 cups all-purpose flour

½ teaspoon salt

1½ cups granulated sugar

1 tablespoon baking powder

½ cup whole milk

½ cup margarita mix (with alcohol)

¼ cup tequila

½ cup vegetable oil

3 large eggs, beaten

1 tablespoon lime zest

1 cup dried mango, cut into pea-sized pieces

FOR THE ICING:

2 cups confectioners' sugar, sifted

¼ cup lime juice

¼ cup dried mango, cut into pea-sized pieces, for decoration

Orange sugar crystals, for decoration

Strawberry Daiquiri Cupcakes

Makes 12

FOR THE CUPCAKES:

½ cup strawberries
(fresh or frozen and thawed),
finely chopped

½ cup dark rum

1 tablespoon plus ¾ cup
granulated sugar

1¼ cups cake flour

¼ teaspoon baking soda

¾ teaspoon baking powder

¼ teaspoon salt

6 tablespoons salted butter, at room
temperature

2 large eggs

¼ cup buttermilk

FOR THE WHIPPED CREAM:

½ cup heavy cream

2 tablespoons granulated sugar

1 teaspoon dark rum

THESE CUPCAKES ARE BEST MADE IN LATE SPRING, EARLY summer, when strawberries are at their freshest and flavors are most intense. Fresh from the farmers' market or grocer's freezer, the smell of strawberries baking beats any cheap candle by a long shot. And why buy whipped cream when you can make it fresh with this easy recipe?

1. Preheat the oven to 350°F. Line a cupcake pan with 12 cupcake liners. Set aside.

2. In a small saucepan, heat the strawberries, rum, and 1 tablespoon sugar over medium heat. Stir until the liquid is absorbed, about 10 minutes. Set aside to cool.

3. In a medium bowl, sift together the cake flour, baking soda, baking powder, and salt. Set aside.

4. In a large bowl, use an electric mixer on medium-high speed to beat the butter until creamy. Add the remaining ¾ cup sugar, beating until light and fluffy. Add the eggs, one at a time. Slowly mix in the cooled strawberry mixture. Turn the mixer to low and alternate between adding the buttermilk and the flour mixture in four batches, ending with the flour, and scraping the bowl as necessary. Beat just until combined.

5. Divide the batter evenly among the cupcake liners and bake for 16 to 20 minutes, or until a toothpick inserted into the center of the cupcake comes out clean. Cool on a wire rack for 5 minutes, or until cool enough to handle. Remove the cupcakes from the pan and cool completely.

6. Make the whipped cream no more than 3 hours before serving. To make the whipped cream, use the electric mixer on medium-high speed to whisk the cream until it is slightly thick. Gradually add the sugar and rum and continue beating until soft peaks form. Do not overbeat or the cream will curdle. Dollop the whipped cream onto the cupcakes.

Top o' the Morning Cupcakes

Makes 24

FOR THE CUPCAKES:

2 cups all-purpose flour

1¾ cups granulated sugar

¾ cup cocoa powder

½ teaspoon salt

1 tablespoon baking soda

1 large egg

⅔ cup oil

¾ cup buttermilk

¼ cup Irish cream liqueur

1 cup black coffee, at room temperature

FOR THE ICING:

2 teaspoons instant coffee granules

½ cup Irish cream liqueur, warm

4 ounces (1 stick) salted butter, at room temperature

1 teaspoon vanilla extract

¼ teaspoon salt

3½ cups confectioners' sugar, sifted

½ cup chocolate sprinkles or mini chocolate chips, for topping

WHAT?! YOU'VE NEVER HAD A CUPCAKE FOR BREAKFAST?! Well, now's the time! These rich cupcakes will start your morning on the right foot. And really, how can you go wrong with a cupcake featuring the superbly wonderful combination of coffee and chocolate?

1. Preheat the oven to 350°F. Line a cupcake pan with 24 cupcake liners. Set aside.

2. In a medium bowl, sift together the flour, sugar, cocoa powder, salt, and baking soda. Set aside.

3. In a large bowl, beat together the egg, oil, buttermilk, Irish cream liqueur, and coffee.

4. Use an electric mixer on medium speed and slowly add the flour mixture to the egg mixture, beating for 2 to 3 minutes or just until the flour is incorporated.

5. Pour the batter into the prepared cups. Bake for 15 to 17 minutes, or until a toothpick inserted into the center of the cupcake comes out clean. Cool on a wire rack for 5 minutes, or until cool enough to handle. Remove the cupcakes from the pan and cool completely.

6. For the icing, dissolve the coffee granules in the warm Irish cream liqueur and set aside.

7. In a medium bowl, use the electric mixer on medium-high speed to cream the butter, gradually adding the vanilla and salt. Slowly add the sugar and enough of the Irish cream liqueur mixture to create a smooth and fluffy frosting.

8. Place the icing in a large freezer storage bag with a small hole cut in one corner. Use this bag to pipe the icing onto the cooled cupcakes. Decorate each cupcake with a teaspoon of chocolate sprinkles or mini chocolate chips.

White Chocolate and Raspberry Cupcakes

Makes 24

FOR THE CUPCAKES:

2 cups all-purpose flour

3½ teaspoons baking powder

¼ teaspoon salt

1 cup granulated sugar

4 large eggs

8 ounces (2 sticks) unsalted butter, at room temperature

½ cup raspberry liqueur

½ cup white chocolate chips

FOR THE ICING:

1 (8-ounce) package cream cheese, at room temperature

3 tablespoons salted butter, at room temperature

1½ cups confectioners' sugar, sifted

½ teaspoon vanilla extract

¼ cup frozen raspberries, thawed and chopped

THESE ARE LOVELY LITTLE CUPCAKES WITH A BURST OF FLAVOR from the bright red raspberries. The slight tang of the fruit makes for the perfect balance in the sweet icing. Delish!

1. Preheat the oven to 350°F. Line a cupcake pan with 24 cupcake liners. Set aside.

2. In a medium bowl, combine the flour, baking powder, salt, and sugar. Set aside.

3. Combine the eggs, butter, liqueur, and chocolate chips in a large bowl. Use an electric mixer on medium speed and blend for 2 to 3 minutes, or until light and creamy. Turn the mixer to medium-low speed and add the flour mixture, blending just until combined.

4. Pour the batter into the prepared cups. Bake for 18 to 22 minutes, or until a toothpick inserted into the center of the cupcake comes out clean. Cool on a wire rack for 5 minutes, or until cool enough to handle. Remove the cupcakes from the pan and cool completely.

5. For the icing, use the mixer on medium-high speed to beat the cream cheese and butter until well mixed. Slowly add the sugar and vanilla, and beat until smooth and fluffy. Turn the mixer to low and add the chopped raspberries.

6. When the cupcakes are cool, decorate them with icing.

FUN STUFF

<hr/>

KATHARINE HEPBURN ONCE SAID THAT IF YOU OBEY ALL THE rules, you miss all the fun, but this section conjures up a cornucopia of cupcake recipes that implores you to follow the rules *and* have a good time! These are the party cupcakes, the ones that will guarantee you a spot on everyone's guest list. From brandied apples, doused in enough booze to make your granny blush, to rum-soaked raisins that turn a traditional carrot cake from healthy to hedonistic, this is the section where you say *so what* to calories, *who cares* to caution, and *why not* to letting your hair down and having a good time. And while it may seem weird to include something "dark and stormy" in Fun Stuff, you have to remember that every cloud has a silver lining, with this cupcake's shining spotlight firmly fixed on a hearty dose of ginger beer. So, flick through these recipes, throw on your favorite apron, and have yourself a little kitchen dance party.

Bloody Mary Cupcakes

BLOODY MARY CUPCAKES ARE THE PERFECT LITTLE SNACK FOR a Sunday morning brunch. Made with tomato soup, Tabasco® sauce, and Worcestershire sauce, they are unlike any cupcakes you have ever had. They should be made according to your own taste—if you like your drink spicier, add more spice. Go crazy with gummy candy on toothpicks for absolutely showstopping cupcakes.

1. Preheat the oven to 350°F. Line a cupcake pan with 12 cupcake liners. Set aside.

2. In a medium bowl, combine the flour, baking soda, cinnamon, celery salt, and black pepper. Set aside.

3. In a large bowl, use an electric mixer on medium speed to beat the butter lightly. Add the sugar, mixing lightly. Add the eggs, beating until light and fluffy. Add the Tabasco, Worcestershire, vodka, and food coloring, mixing until well combined. Alternate between adding the soup and flour mixtures in four additions, ending with the flour mixture.

4. Divide the batter evenly among the cupcake liners and bake for 18 to 22 minutes, or until a toothpick inserted into the center of the cupcake comes out clean. Cool on a wire rack for 5 minutes, or until cool enough to handle. Remove the cupcakes from the pan and cool completely.

5. For the glaze, mix the sugar, lime juice, and vodka with a fork. Drizzle the glaze onto the cooled cupcakes and immediately top with a small pinch of sea salt.

Makes 12

FOR THE CUPCAKES:

2 cups all-purpose flour

¾ teaspoon baking soda

1 teaspoon ground cinnamon

1 teaspoon celery salt

½ teaspoon freshly ground black pepper

4 ounces (1 stick) salted butter, at room temperature

1⅛ cups light brown sugar, packed

2 large eggs

1½ teaspoons Tabasco® sauce

¼ teaspoon Worcestershire sauce

¼ cup vodka

1½ teaspoons red food coloring

¾ cup condensed tomato soup

FOR THE GLAZE:

½ cup confectioners' sugar, sifted

1 tablespoon lime juice

1 tablespoon vodka

2 teaspoons sea salt, for dusting

Bright and Cheery Orange Raspberry Cupcakes

Makes 18

FOR THE CANDIED ORANGE PEEL:

Peel of 2 oranges

¾ cup granulated sugar

FOR THE CUPCAKES:

1 (18.25-ounce) box yellow cake mix

1 (5-ounce) package instant vanilla pudding mix

½ cup orange juice

4 large eggs

⅓ cup vegetable oil

2 tablespoons triple sec

FOR THE GLAZE:

6 tablespoons unsalted butter

2 cups confectioners' sugar, sifted

1½ teaspoons triple sec

½ cup frozen raspberries, thawed and mashed

BRIGHT PINKS AND ORANGES MAKE THESE CUPCAKES AN undeniably fitting addition to any picnic or barbecue. A topping made of candied orange peel gives the cupcakes a little something extra. Go that extra step and add a paper umbrella.

1. Preheat the oven to 350°F. Line a cupcake pan with 18 cupcake liners. Set aside.

2. Begin by making the candied orange peel. Use a vegetable peeler to cut long ¾-inch-wide orange strips. Drop the orange strips in ¾ cup of boiling water for 1 minute, and then rinse the strips under cold water. Heat ½ cup of fresh water with the sugar on medium-high until the sugar dissolves. Bring to a boil. Add the orange peels and simmer in the sugar and water until tender, about 15 minutes. Use a fork to remove the peels and place them on a sheet of parchment paper to dry for about 1 hour.

3. While the peels are drying, make the cupcakes. In a large bowl, use an electric mixer on medium speed to beat the cake and pudding mixes, orange juice, eggs, vegetable oil, and triple sec until smooth, 3 to 5 minutes.

(continued)

4. Pour the batter into the prepared cups. Bake for 18 to 22 minutes, or until a toothpick inserted into the center of the cupcake comes out clean. Cool on a wire rack for 5 minutes, or until cool enough to handle. Remove the cupcakes from the pan and cool completely.

5. For the glaze, melt the butter in a saucepan. Stir in the sugar and triple sec and mix until smooth. Add the raspberries and their juice to this mixture. Stir until thick. Drizzle the glaze onto the cooled cupcakes and immediately top with the cooled orange peels.

KATE'S TIP: For cupcakes with a tangier zing, substitute the peel of four large limes for the orange peel.

Car Bomb Cupcakes

WHISKEY? CHECK. GUINNESS®? CHECK. BAILEYS®? CHECK.
*Deliciousness? You betcha. These cupcakes have it all, and your friends are sure to
love the surprise whiskey bombs hidden inside. Made with rich chocolate ganache,
these cupcakes will remind you that sometimes hidden surprises are a really good
thing. You'll be seeing leprechauns dancing beneath rainbows in no time!*

1. Preheat the oven to 350°F. Line a cupcake pan with 12 cupcake liners. Set aside.

2. In a medium saucepan, heat the Guinness and butter over medium heat, stirring until the butter melts. Add the cocoa, stirring until smooth. Set aside to cool.

3. In a medium bowl, sift together the flour, sugar, baking soda, and salt. Set aside.

4. In a large bowl, use an electric mixer on medium speed to beat together the egg and sour cream until smooth. Continue beating as you add the cooled Guinness mixture. Turn the mixer to low and add the flour mixture, beating just until combined.

5. Divide the batter evenly among the cupcake liners and bake for 16 to 20 minutes, or until a toothpick inserted into the center of the cupcake comes out clean. Cool on a wire rack for 5 minutes, or until cool enough to handle. Remove the cupcakes from the pan and cool completely.

(continued)

Makes 12

FOR THE CUPCAKES:

½ cup Guinness®

4 ounces (1 stick) salted butter

⅓ cup unsweetened cocoa powder

1 cup all-purpose flour

1 cup granulated sugar

¾ teaspoon baking soda

½ teaspoon salt

1 large egg

⅓ cup sour cream

FOR THE WHISKEY GANACHE:

4 ounces dark chocolate, chopped into pieces no bigger than 1 × 1 inch

⅓ cup heavy cream

1 tablespoon unsalted butter, at room temperature

4 teaspoons whiskey

6. For the ganache, place the chocolate pieces in a heatproof bowl. Heat the cream in a saucepan on low heat, stirring until simmering. Pour the cream over the chocolate, stirring constantly. Add the butter and whiskey, stirring until smooth. Set aside, but stir every couple of minutes until the mixture thickens, about 20 minutes.

7. While you let the ganache cool and the cupcakes have cooled completely, use a knife or star-shaped piping tip to cut a hole in the top of each cupcake about two-thirds of the way down, making room for about 1 tablespoon of ganache. Use a piping bag or a sandwich bag with a hole cut in the corner to fill the cupcake hole with the thickened ganache.

8. For the icing, use the mixer on medium-high speed to cream the butter in a large bowl, gradually adding the vanilla and salt. Slowly add the sugar, mixing until smooth. Add the Baileys to create a smooth and fluffy frosting and pipe the frosting onto the cooled cupcakes.

FOR THE ICING:

4 tablespoons salted butter, at room temperature

¾ teaspoon vanilla extract

Dash of salt

2 cups confectioners' sugar, sifted

¼ cup Baileys® Irish Cream

Dark and Stormy Cupcakes

GINGER IS A BIT OF AN OBSESSION OF MINE, WITH ITS CONFIDENT yet delicate kick. Add some rum to that ginger and you've got a drink worth sticking with all night . . . and a cupcake to match! And did someone mention chocolate? I'll take twelve, please!

1. Preheat the oven to 350°F. Line a cupcake pan with 12 cupcake liners. Set aside.

2. Heat the butter, ginger beer, and rum over low heat for about 3 minutes, until the butter melts, being careful not to boil. Set aside.

3. Sift together the cocoa powder, cinnamon, ginger, flour, sugar, and salt.

4. In a small bowl, beat together the egg, buttermilk, and baking soda.

5. Stir the warm butter mixture into the sifted ingredients. Add the egg mixture and stir until well combined.

6. Divide the batter evenly among the cupcake liners and bake for 16 to 20 minutes, or until a toothpick inserted into the center of the cupcake comes out clean. Cool on a wire rack for 5 minutes, or until cool enough to handle. Remove the cupcakes from the pan and cool completely.

7. For the icing, use an electric mixer to beat the cream cheese and butter until light and fluffy, about 5 minutes. Slowly add the sugar, ground ginger, and rum. Use the mixer on medium-high speed and beat until smooth and fluffy. Smooth the icing onto the cooled cupcakes and garnish with the candied ginger.

Makes 12

FOR THE CUPCAKES:

4 ounces (1 stick) salted butter

½ cup ginger beer
(the stronger, the better)

¼ cup dark rum

2 tablespoons cocoa powder

1 teaspoon ground cinnamon

1 teaspoon ground ginger

1½ cups all-purpose flour, sifted

1 cup granulated sugar

¼ teaspoon salt

1 large egg, beaten

¼ cup buttermilk

½ teaspoon baking soda

FOR THE ICING:

1 (8-ounce) package cream cheese,
at room temperature

4 tablespoons unsalted butter,
at room temperature

1 cup confectioners' sugar, sifted

2 teaspoons ground ginger

1 tablespoon dark rum

¼ cup candied ginger, for garnish

Spiked Eggnog Cupcakes

Makes 12

FOR THE CUPCAKES:

1½ cups cake flour

1¼ teaspoons baking powder

¼ teaspoon salt

4 tablespoons unsalted butter,
at room temperature

¾ cup granulated sugar

1 large egg

2 tablespoons dark rum

½ teaspoon vanilla extract

¾ cup eggnog

FOR THE GLAZE:

1½ teaspoons light corn syrup

¾ cup confectioners' sugar, sifted

2 tablespoons eggnog

1 teaspoon ground nutmeg,
for dusting

SWEETS AND BOOZE CAN MAKE DIFFICULT FAMILY FUNCTIONS bearable and pleasant family functions just glorious! These eggnog cupcakes, mistletoe, and some classic Bing Crosby tunes are all you really need to get a holiday party started. Oh, and it's pretty much mandatory that you play Christmas carols as these bake—while drinking your own glass of boozy eggnog!

1. Preheat the oven to 350°F. Line a cupcake pan with 12 cupcake liners. Set aside.

2. Sift together the flour, baking powder, and salt. Set aside.

3. In a large bowl, use an electric mixer on medium-high speed and beat the butter until creamy. Add the sugar and beat until light and fluffy. Continue beating as you add the egg. Once smooth, add the rum, vanilla, and eggnog.

4. Turn the mixer to medium-low speed and add the dry mixture, beating just until combined.

5. Divide the mixture evenly between the baking cups.

6. Bake for 18 to 22 minutes, or until a toothpick inserted into the center of the cupcake comes out clean. Cool on a wire rack for 5 minutes, or until cool enough to handle. Remove the cupcakes from the pan and cool completely.

7. For the glaze, mix the corn syrup, sugar, and eggnog in a small bowl with a fork. Spoon the icing onto the cooled cupcakes. Top with a dusting of nutmeg.

KATE'S TIP: Feeling like you're about to spill over with holiday cheer? Go all out and express your merriment through an alternative topping. While nutmeg is the traditional eggnog topping, crushed candy canes add a bit of texture and a crisp peppermint scent atop the glaze.

Minty Mojito Cupcakes

Makes 12

FOR THE CUPCAKES:

1 cup all-purpose flour

1 teaspoon baking powder

½ teaspoon salt

4 ounces (1 stick) unsalted butter, at room temperature

1 cup granulated sugar

2 large eggs

3 tablespoons dark rum

Zest from 1 lime

½ cup mint, finely chopped (by hand or food processor)

½ cup sour cream

FOR THE ICING:

5 tablespoons unsalted butter, at room temperature

1½ teaspoons dark rum

1 tablespoon whole milk

1 tablespoon mint, finely chopped

1 tablespoon lime juice

2 cups confectioners' sugar, sifted

2 to 4 drops green food coloring

Zest from 1 lime, for garnish

MINTY MOJITO CUPCAKES ARE SUREFIRE CROWD PLEASERS, with that distinctly refreshing mint and lime combo. They have a delicate flavor that will have you coming back for seconds and thirds. Perfect for a summer barbecue or maybe just a cold day where you'd prefer to dream of warm summer vacations.

1. Preheat the oven to 325°F. Line a cupcake pan with 12 cupcake liners. Set aside.

2. In a medium bowl, sift together the flour, baking powder, and salt. Set aside.

3. In a large bowl, use an electric mixer on high speed to cream the butter and sugar together until light and fluffy, about 5 minutes. Add the eggs, one at a time, scraping down the sides of the bowl after each addition. Continue beating as you add the rum, lime zest, and mint.

4. Alternate between adding the flour mixture and sour cream in three additions.

5. Divide the batter evenly among the cupcake liners and bake for 15 to 18 minutes, or until a toothpick inserted into the center of the cupcake comes out clean. Cool on a wire rack for 5 minutes, or until cool enough to handle. Remove the cupcakes from the pan and cool completely.

(continued)

6. For the icing, use the mixer to beat the butter, rum, milk, mint, and lime juice until well mixed. Slowly add the sugar. Turn the mixer to medium-high and beat until smooth and fluffy. Add the green food coloring until the mixture becomes a delicate light green color. Place the icing in the fridge to firm up for about 10 minutes. This will make piping it a bit easier.

7. Smooth or pipe the icing onto the cooled cupcakes and garnish with the lime zest.

> **KATE'S TIP:** Strolling through the candy store can be a great source for cupcake topping inspiration. Depending on what's available in your local penny candy aisle, gummy mint leaves or gummy lime slices would look adorable atop these cupcakes.

Tooty-Fruity Sangria Cupcakes

THESE FRUITY SANGRIA CUPCAKES WILL MAKE A REAL SPLASH at your next fiesta. Chunks of real fruit add an authentic flair to these moist cupcakes. Sombrero: optional. Olé!

1. Preheat the oven to 350°F. Line a cupcake pan with 24 cupcake liners. Set aside.

2. In a large bowl, use an electric mixer on medium speed to mix all of the cupcake ingredients, except the fruit cocktail, until well combined. Add the fruit cocktail, mixing just until combined.

3. Divide the batter evenly among the cupcake liners and bake for 16 to 20 minutes, or until a toothpick inserted into the center of the cupcake comes out clean. Cool on a wire rack for 5 minutes, or until cool enough to handle. Remove the cupcakes from the pan and cool completely.

4. For the icing, use the mixer on medium speed to beat the butter until light and fluffy. Add the marmalade, mixing until well combined. Gradually add the sugar, beating until smooth. Add the remaining ingredients and mix until light and fluffy. Smooth the icing onto the cooled cupcakes.

Makes 24

FOR THE CUPCAKES:

1 (18.25-ounce) box yellow cake mix

1 (5-ounce) package instant vanilla pudding mix

¾ cup vegetable oil

¾ cup red wine

4 large eggs

1 tablespoon red food coloring

1 cup canned fruit cocktail, drained

FOR THE ICING:

8 ounces (2 sticks) salted butter, at room temperature

⅔ cup chunky marmalade

3 cups confectioners' sugar, sifted

2 tablespoons heavy cream

1 teaspoon vanilla extract

1 teaspoon orange extract

2 teaspoons red wine

Not Your Granny's Apple Cupcakes

Makes 12

¼ cup brandy

3 tablespoons plus ½ cup granulated sugar

1 small red apple, thinly sliced

4 ounces (1 stick) salted butter, at room temperature

1 cup all-purpose flour

1½ teaspoons baking powder

½ teaspoon salt

2 large eggs

¾ cup unsweetened applesauce

1 teaspoon ground cinnamon

½ cup chopped pecans

2 tablespoon coarse raw sugar, for sprinkling

IT MAY SMELL LIKE GRANDMA'S KITCHEN WHEN YOU BAKE THESE aroma-inducing cupcakes, but the brandied apples that lay on top would make most grannies blush. These warm cupcakes are the perfect accessory for your summer picnic—and even more delectable when paired with a bowlful of cold French vanilla ice cream!

1. Preheat the oven to 350°F. Line a cupcake pan with 12 cupcake liners. Set aside.

2. In a medium pan, combine the brandy and 3 tablespoons sugar over low heat, stirring continuously. After 3 minutes, add the sliced apple. Continue stirring for 2 minutes. Remove from the heat, separate the apple from the brandy, and set each aside.

3. In a large bowl, use an electric mixer on medium speed to beat together the butter, the remaining ½ cup sugar, flour, baking powder, salt, and eggs until pale and well combined, about 2 minutes. Turn the mixer down to low speed and stir in the applesauce, prepared brandy, cinnamon, and pecans. Spoon the batter into the prepared cups.

4. Lay several thin slices of the apple on each cupcake and sprinkle the coarse sugar on top.

5. Bake for 22 to 25 minutes, or until a toothpick inserted into the center of the cupcake comes out clean. Cool on a wire rack for 5 minutes, or until cool enough to handle. Remove the cupcakes from the pan and serve while still warm.

Rum and Carrot Cupcakes

CARROT CAKE IS SUCH A TRADITIONAL CAKE THAT I THOUGHT it was high time it got a little kick in the bum. Rum-soaked raisins and carrots do an expert job of adding a bit of an edge to an old standby.

1. Preheat the oven to 350°F. Line a cupcake pan with 12 cupcake liners. Set aside.

2. In a medium bowl, sift together the flour, baking powder, salt, cinnamon, and nutmeg. Set aside.

3. In a medium saucepan, mix together the raisins, carrots, rum, and orange juice over low heat. Stir as the mixture simmers for 5 minutes. Remove from the heat.

4. In a large bowl, use an electric mixer on medium speed to beat the eggs and sugar until creamy. Add the vegetable oil and continue beating. Add the raisin mixture (including the rum they were cooked in) and the walnuts while beating. Turn the mixer to low and add the dry ingredients, mixing until combined.

5. Divide the batter evenly among the cupcake liners and bake for 18 to 22 minutes, or until a toothpick inserted into the center of the cupcake comes out clean. Cool on a wire rack for 5 minutes, or until cool enough to handle. Remove the cupcakes from the pan and cool completely.

(continued)

Makes 12

FOR THE CUPCAKES:

1¼ cups all-purpose flour

2 teaspoons baking powder

½ teaspoon salt

1 teaspoon ground cinnamon

½ teaspoon ground nutmeg

½ cup raisins

1½ cups carrots, grated

¼ cup orange rum

1 tablespoon orange juice

2 large eggs

1 cup granulated sugar

½ cup vegetable oil

⅓ cup walnuts, chopped

FOR THE ICING:

1 (8-ounce) package cream cheese, at room temperature

7 tablespoons unsalted butter, at room temperature

2 cups confectioners' sugar, sifted

2 tablespoons rum

¼ cup chopped walnuts, for garnish

6. For the icing, use the mixer to beat the cream cheese and butter until light and fluffy, about 5 minutes. Slowly add the sugar and rum. Beat on medium-high until smooth and fluffy. Dollop the icing onto the cooled cupcakes and garnish with the chopped walnuts.

KATE'S TIP: Not a fan of nuts? Don't get your panties in a bunch. Substitute the walnuts with half a cup of chocolate chips.

FANCY STUFF

❦

OUR LIVES ARE FULL OF SPECIAL OCCASIONS: FINDING THE perfect pair of shoes, for example, or the blind date that actually goes well. If you have such an occasion, or a friend's birthday or bridal shower, for that matter, put on your high heels, pull out your reddest lipstick, and start pouring the batter. These tasty treats are for those special moments when only a boozy cupcake will do, the kind of occasion that cries out for Champagne. The kinds of occasions when toasts are given, gifts are exchanged, and mascara is smudged. From Belgian fruit beers to Japanese sake, these cupcakes also take on a continental flair, adding more panache to the fanciful nature of the recipes. From the chichi Wine and Cheese Party Cupcakes to the spiffy Bellini Belle Cupcakes, these elegant and decadent cupcakes are fit for your fanciest of fancy occasions. Also, wearing pearls as you pour the batter is encouraged, but optional.

Belgian Beauty Cupcakes

HOW CAN YOU GO WRONG WITH A COUNTRY KNOWN FOR ITS beer, chocolate, and waffles? These cupcakes are dedicated to the great country of Belgium. If you haven't tried Belgium's fruity lambic beers, well, today is the day, sister. Framboise lambic beer is fermented using raspberries. This beer and the rich dark Belgian chocolate come together beautifully in these decadent cupcakes that will have you packing your bags for Europe and practicing, "Une bière, s'il vous plaît!"

1. Preheat the oven to 350°F. Line a cupcake pan with 12 cupcake liners. Set aside.

2. In a large bowl, sift together the flour, baking soda, salt, sugar, and cocoa. Add the shortening in small pieces, and then add the buttermilk and framboise beer. Use an electric mixer on low speed to mix for several minutes, scraping the bowl as needed. Add the egg and yolk, beating for an additional 2 minutes, or until well combined. Stir in the chopped chocolate.

3. Divide the batter evenly among the cupcake liners and bake for 16 to 20 minutes, or until a toothpick inserted into the center of the cupcake comes out clean. Cool on a wire rack for 5 minutes, or until cool enough to handle. Remove the cupcakes from the pan and cool completely.

(continued)

Makes 12

FOR THE CUPCAKES:

1 cup all-purpose flour

¾ teaspoon baking soda

½ teaspoon salt

¾ cup granulated sugar

¼ cup cocoa powder

¼ cup butter-flavored shortening

⅓ cup buttermilk

¼ cup Belgian framboise beer

1 large egg

1 egg yolk from a large egg

⅔ cup dark Belgian chocolate, chopped into pieces no bigger than 1 × 1 inch

FOR THE ICING:

1 cup dark Belgian chocolate, chopped into pieces no bigger than 1 × 1 inch

5 tablespoons unsalted butter, at room temperature

1 tablespoon Belgian framboise beer

12 raspberries, for garnish

4. For the icing, heat the chocolate pieces at a low temperature in a double boiler (see page 14). Stir until three-quarters of the chocolate is melted. Remove from the heat and continue stirring, and allow the chocolate to cool completely.

5. In a medium bowl, use the mixer to beat the butter until light and fluffy. Add the framboise beer and gradually beat in the cooled chocolate, beating until thick and creamy. Dollop the icing onto the cupcakes and top each with a raspberry.

KATE'S TIP: If you can't find Belgian chocolate, use another high-quality dark chocolate instead.

Bellini Belle Cupcakes

THERE'S SOMETHING SO CLASSY ABOUT DRINKING A TALL bubbly Bellini. *A drink so elegant, it brings out the Audrey Hepburn in us all. It's fitting, then, that these cupcakes have a satiny icing, fit for a starlet.*

1. Preheat the oven to 350°F. Line a cupcake pan with 16 cupcake liners. Set aside.

2. In a clean large bowl, use an electric mixer to beat the egg whites until stiff peaks form. Set aside.

3. In another large bowl, cream the butter and sugar until light and fluffy. Sift together the flour, baking powder, and salt. Alternate between adding the flour mixture and Champagne into the butter mixture. Stir in the chopped peaches.

4. Fold one-third of the egg whites into the batter, and then fold in the remaining two-thirds.

5. Pour the batter into the prepared cups. Bake for 18 to 22 minutes, or until a toothpick inserted into the center of the cupcake comes out clean. Cool on a wire rack for 5 minutes, or until cool enough to handle. Remove the cupcakes from the pan and cool completely.

6. For the icing, mix the gelatin and Champagne over low heat in a medium saucepan. Stir until simmering and remove from the heat.

7. In a large bowl, use the mixer on medium speed to beat the butter until light in color. Add the gelatin mixture, sugar, and enough food coloring for a peachy orange color. Mix until light and fluffy and spread the icing onto the cooled cupcakes.

Makes 16

FOR THE CUPCAKES:

6 egg whites from large eggs

5 ounces (1¼ sticks) unsalted butter, at room temperature

1½ cups granulated sugar

2 cups all-purpose flour

1 tablespoon baking powder

1 teaspoon salt

¾ cup Champagne (or sparkling wine)

⅔ cup canned peaches, chopped

FOR THE ICING:

1 (4-ounce) package peach-flavored gelatin

½ cup Champagne

4 ounces (1 stick) unsalted butter, at room temperature

4½ cups confectioners' sugar, sifted

8 to 10 drops orange food coloring

Champagne Party Cupcakes

THESE FLIRTY CUPCAKES ARE COLORFUL AND DELICATE AND pack their very own little party. They have a light pink glaze and a surprising burst of color when bitten into. Perfect for bachelorette parties, bridal showers, or any call for a celebration at all!

1. Preheat the oven to 350°F. Line a cupcake pan with 16 cupcake liners. Set aside.

2. In a clean large bowl, beat the egg whites until stiff peaks form. Set aside.

3. In a large bowl, cream the butter and sugar until light and fluffy. Sift together the flour, baking powder, and salt. Alternate between adding the flour mixture and Champagne into the butter mixture. Stir in the confetti.

4. Fold one-third of the egg whites into the batter. Then fold in the remaining two-thirds of the egg whites.

5. Pour the batter into the prepared cups. Bake for 18 to 22 minutes, or until a toothpick inserted into the center of the cupcake comes out clean. Cool on a wire rack for 5 minutes, or until cool enough to handle. Remove the cupcakes from the pan and cool completely.

(continued)

Makes 16

FOR THE CUPCAKES:

6 egg whites from large eggs

5 ounces (1¼ sticks) unsalted butter, at room temperature

1½ cups granulated sugar

2⅔ cups all-purpose flour

1 tablespoon baking powder

1 teaspoon salt

¾ cup Champagne (or sparkling wine)

¼ cup colorful confetti sprinkles

FOR THE GLAZE:

1½ cups confectioners' sugar, sifted

6 to 8 drops pink food coloring

5 tablespoons Champagne

3 tablespoons colorful confetti sprinkles, for decoration

6. For the glaze, mix the sugar, food coloring, and Champagne in a small bowl. Drizzle the glaze onto the cooled cupcakes and immediately decorate with the confetti sprinkles.

KATE'S TIP: For a fancier presentation, why not make these in a mini cupcake pan and sit the tiny cupcakes atop tall Champagne glasses? Super classy.

Chocolate Grand Marnier® Cupcakes

CHOCOLATE AND ORANGE. MMMM MMM MMMMM! *THE CITRUS scent hits your nose just as the cupcakes reach your lips. The orange flavors add a refreshing twist to a deliciously moist chocolate cupcake. Antioxidant powers galore!*

Makes 18

1. Preheat the oven to 350°F. Line a cupcake pan with 18 cupcake liners. Set aside.

2. In a large bowl, sift together the flour, sugar, cocoa, baking soda, and salt. With an electric mixer on low speed, slowly add the oil and vanilla until fully incorporated.

3. Gradually add the coffee and Grand Marnier. The mixture will separate and then come back together to form a smooth consistency. Add the vinegar, mixing just until combined.

4. Divide the batter evenly among the cupcake liners. Bake for 16 to 20 minutes, or until a toothpick inserted into the center of the cupcake comes out clean. Cool on a wire rack for 5 minutes, or until cool enough to handle. Remove the cupcakes from the pan and cool completely.

5. For the icing, heat the chocolate chips at a low temperature in a double boiler (see page 14). Stir until three-quarters of the chocolate is melted. Remove from the heat and continue stirring. Allow the chocolate to cool completely while stirring.

6. In a bowl, beat the butter until light and fluffy. Add the Grand Marnier. Gradually beat in the cooled chocolate, beating until thick and creamy. Dollop the icing onto the cooled cupcakes and top with the orange zest.

FOR THE CUPCAKES:

2¼ cups all-purpose flour

1½ cups granulated sugar

½ cup cocoa powder

1½ teaspoons baking soda

1 teaspoon salt

¾ cup vegetable oil

1 tablespoon vanilla extract

1½ cups strong coffee, at room temperature

½ cup Grand Marnier®

2 tablespoons cider vinegar

FOR THE ICING:

1½ cups semisweet chocolate chips

4 ounces (1 stick) unsalted butter, at room temperature

2 tablespoons Grand Marnier®, warm

Zest from 1 large orange, for garnish

Fancy Pants
Golden Gingerbread Cupcakes

IF GOLDEN CUPCAKES DON'T IMPRESS YOUR GUESTS, THEN I don't know what will. As a young girl, I was always fascinated by my parents' Goldschläger® drinks. I couldn't wait until I was an adult and could drink my very own gold. Well, now is your chance to eat and drink some of the big-kid stuff. Perfect for a very special event!

1. Preheat the oven to 350°F. Line a cupcake pan with 12 cupcake liners. Set aside.

2. Pour the Goldschläger through a coffee filter, reserving the gold bits for the glaze. Set both aside.

3. In a medium bowl, sift together the flour, ginger, cinnamon, baking soda, and salt. Set aside.

4. In a large bowl, combine the sugar, buttermilk, molasses, melted butter, eggs, and the sieved Goldschläger. Add the flour mixture and stir until combined.

5. Divide the batter evenly among the cupcake liners and bake for 18 to 22 minutes, or until a toothpick inserted into the center of the cupcake comes out clean. Cool on a wire rack for 5 minutes, or until cool enough to handle. Remove the cupcakes from the pan and cool completely.

(continued)

Makes 12

FOR THE CUPCAKES:

½ cup Goldschläger®

1½ cups all-purpose flour

2 teaspoons ground ginger

1½ teaspoons ground cinnamon

¾ teaspoon baking soda

¼ teaspoon salt

½ cup light brown sugar, packed

½ cup buttermilk

½ cup dark molasses

5 tablespoons unsalted butter, melted

2 large eggs, lightly beaten

FOR THE GLAZE:

2 tablespoons unsalted butter, melted

½ cup confectioners' sugar, sifted

2 tablespoons Goldschläger®

6. For the glaze, combine the melted butter, sugar, and Goldschläger with a fork. Drizzle the glaze over the cupcakes. Use a toothpick to scrape the captured gold from the coffee filter and add a touch of this gold to the top of each cupcake.

KATE'S TIP: These days, you can find just about any style of cupcake wrapper. Why not use a metallic gold liner for these cupcakes to give them a bit of extra bling? Use the wrapper template on page 122 to make your very own.

Naked Geisha Cupcakes

*EXPRESS YOUR INNER GEISHA WITH THESE CLASSY AND EXOTIC
cupcakes, with some unexpected flavors. Candied ginger and a hint of sake
gives your traditional chocolate cupcakes a well-needed kick in the bum. Go
bottomless and leave your cupcake liners at home!*

1. Preheat the oven to 350°F. Spray a cupcake pan with butter-flavored cooking spray. Sprinkle the 4 tablespoons of sugar into the cups and rotate the pan to ensure that each cup is evenly coated. Set aside.

2. In a large bowl, sift together the flour, cocoa, coffee, baking soda, salt, and cinnamon.

3. In another bowl, use an electric mixer on medium-high speed to mix the remaining 2 cups sugar and butter for 3 minutes. Add the eggs, one at a time, beating until incorporated. Mix in the vanilla, milk, and sake.

4. Pour this mixture into the flour mixture and stir, by hand, just until well mixed. Using a large spatula, fold in the chocolate and ginger.

5. Pour the batter into the prepared cups. Bake for 18 to 22 minutes, or until a toothpick inserted into the center of the cupcake comes out clean. Cool on a wire rack for 5 minutes, or until cool enough to handle. Remove the cupcakes from the pan and cool completely.

6. Dust each cupcake with confectioners' sugar.

Makes 12

Butter-flavored cooking spray, for greasing

4 tablespoons plus 2 cups granulated sugar

2 cups all-purpose flour

1 cup unsweetened cocoa powder

2 tablespoons instant coffee granules

1 teaspoon baking soda

½ teaspoon salt

½ teaspoon ground cinnamon

4 ounces (1 stick) unsalted butter, at room temperature

4 large eggs

2 teaspoons vanilla extract

½ cup whole milk

¾ cup sake

⅓ cup bittersweet chocolate, chopped into pea-sized pieces

¾ cup chopped candied ginger

Confectioners' sugar, for dusting

Fiery Red Velvet Cupcakes

Makes 12

FOR THE CUPCAKES:

1¼ cups all-purpose flour

¾ cup granulated sugar

½ teaspoon baking soda

½ teaspoon salt

1 teaspoon cocoa powder

1½ teaspoons ground cinnamon

¾ cup vegetable oil

½ cup buttermilk, at room temperature

1 large egg, at room temperature

6 to 8 drops red food coloring

½ teaspoon white vinegar

½ teaspoon vanilla extract

¼ cup cinnamon schnapps (the hotter, the better)

FOR THE ICING:

4 ounces cream cheese, at room temperature

4 tablespoons unsalted butter, at room temperature

1 cup confectioners' sugar, sifted

1 tablespoon cinnamon schnapps

12 red cinnamon candies, for decoration

THERE'S SOMETHING INCREDIBLY SEXY ABOUT RED VELVET cake. The "velvet" in the name is due to the, well, velvety texture! These velvety bites have a fiery kick to boot. Good thing we've got a healthy dollop of cream cheese to cool things down a bit. Your mouth will thank you.

1. Preheat the oven to 350°F. Line a cupcake pan with 12 cupcake liners. Set aside.

2. Sift together the flour, sugar, baking soda, salt, and cocoa. Set aside.

3. In a large bowl, use an electric mixer on low speed to beat the remaining cupcake ingredients. Slowly add the dry ingredients and mix just until well combined.

4. Divide the batter evenly among the cupcake liners and bake for 16 to 20 minutes, or until a toothpick inserted into the center of the cupcake comes out clean. Cool on a wire rack for 5 minutes, or until cool enough to handle. Remove the cupcakes from the pan and cool completely.

5. For the icing, use an electric mixer to beat the cream cheese and butter until light and fluffy, about 5 minutes. Slowly add the sugar and schnapps and beat on medium-high speed until smooth and fluffy. Smooth the icing onto the cooled cupcakes and garnish each with a cinnamon candy.

Oh-So-Decadent Pear and Hazelnut Cupcakes

Makes 12

FOR THE CUPCAKES:

½ cup granulated sugar

½ cup light brown sugar

1½ cups all-purpose flour

½ teaspoon salt

½ teaspoon baking soda

1½ teaspoons ground cinnamon

1 teaspoon vanilla extract

2 large eggs, beaten

⅓ cup hazelnut liqueur

2 cups canned pears, drained and chopped into ¼- to ½-inch chunks

FOR THE GANACHE:

¼ cup light corn syrup

¾ cup heavy cream

12 ounces dark chocolate, chopped no bigger than 1 × 1 inch

½ teaspoon hazelnut liqueur

¼ cup hazelnuts, chopped, for garnish

THESE SOPHISTICATED CUPCAKES WILL HAVE YOUR GUESTS begging for the recipe! They are inspired by a drink that a friend of mine serves at her annual Christmas cocktail party. The rich ganache just melts in your mouth. The cupcakes have a very grownup taste and texture, but you're sure to feel like a kid when you go back for seconds and thirds.

1. Preheat the oven to 350°F. Line a cupcake pan with 12 cupcake liners. Set aside.

2. In a medium bowl, sift together the sugars, flour, salt, baking soda, and cinnamon. Set aside. In a large bowl, combine the vanilla, eggs, and liqueur. Use an electric mixer on low speed and add the dry ingredients, mixing just until combined. Stir in the chopped pears by hand.

3. Pour the batter into the prepared cups. Bake for 18 to 22 minutes, or until a toothpick inserted into the center of the cupcake comes out clean. Cool on a wire rack for 5 minutes, or until cool enough to handle. Remove the cupcakes from the pan.

(continued)

4. While the cupcakes are baking, prepare the ganache. Combine the corn syrup and cream in a saucepan. Bring to a simmer, add the chocolate, and stir just until the chocolate melts and is smooth. Remove from the heat and add the liqueur. Stir 2 to 3 minutes, or until the ganache thickens slightly.

5. Pour the ganache onto the warm cupcakes. Immediately after the ganache is poured, sprinkle the cupcakes with the chopped hazelnuts.

KATE'S TIP: For an elegant alternative to the chopped hazelnut topping: After the ganache has been poured and set a few minutes, or until no longer sticky to the touch, hold a doily over each cupcake and dust with confectioners' sugar.

Wine and Cheese Party Cupcakes

NOTHING SAYS SOPHISTICATION LIKE A WINE AND CHEESE party, so turn on some jazz, send out the invites, and surprise your guests with these super-rich, wine-infused cupcakes that won't even stain your teeth!

1. Preheat the oven to 350°F. Line a cupcake pan with 20 cupcake liners. Set aside.

2. In a double boiler (see page 14), melt the unsweetened chocolate and butter, stirring until smooth. Set aside to cool.

3. In a clean bowl, use an electric mixer on medium-high speed to whip the egg whites and cream of tartar until soft peaks form. Continue mixing as you add the 3 tablespoons sugar, whipping until stiff peaks form. Set aside.

4. In a large bowl, turn the mixer to high speed and beat the egg yolks and the remaining ¾ cup sugar for 2 minutes. Slowly mix in the wine, flour, salt, and chocolate chunks. Fold in the cooled chocolate mixture, and then fold in the egg white mixture.

5. Pour the batter into the prepared cups. Bake for 16 to 20 minutes, or until a toothpick inserted into the center of the cupcake comes out clean. Cool on a wire rack for 5 minutes, or until cool enough to handle. Remove the cupcakes from the pan and cool completely.

(continued)

Makes 20

FOR THE CUPCAKES:

10 ounces unsweetened chocolate

6 ounces (1½ sticks) unsalted butter

5 egg whites from large eggs, separated

½ teaspoon cream of tartar

3 tablespoons plus ¾ cup granulated sugar

¾ cup red port wine

½ cup all-purpose flour

¼ teaspoon salt

1 cup chocolate chunks, about 1 × 1 inch

FOR THE ICING:

4 tablespoons unsalted butter, at room temperature

8 ounces mascarpone cheese, at room temperature

3¾ cups confectioners' sugar, sifted

1 teaspoon vanilla extract

1 cup white chocolate, slivered

6. For the icing, use the mixer on medium-high speed to beat the butter and mascarpone cheese until fluffy. Slowly add the sugar and vanilla and continue beating until smooth. Pipe the icing onto the cooled cupcakes and add the slivers of white chocolate on top for garnish.

KATE'S TIP: Mini cupcakes are a super-cute party favor. You can make about three times the number of mini cupcakes from the same recipe.

HARD STUFF

—✦—

THERE ARE SOME TIPPLES YOU ONLY INDULGE IN AT OPPORTUNE times: the Irish stout on St. Patrick's Day; the end of the evening bourbon; and the pre-gaming Jäger® bombs that get an evening going. Heck, even the ubiquitous Cosmo is something you only drink on special occasions. These tipples consist of the hard stuff, the stuff that seems like a good idea at the time, even though it may not settle in your stomach the way you want it to. In an intoxicated cupcake recipe, however, the hard stuff sits perfectly. So, roll up your sleeves and roll out the shot glasses. The cupcakes in Hard Stuff are perfect for a little pre-gaming before a night out and great for a nightcap when you stumble back in. They are a little bit naughty and a lot-a-bit tasty. And if you're taking a shot or two of the booze while you bake, watch out—it could get dangerous!

A Bit o' Southern Pride Cupcakes

Makes 16

FOR THE CUPCAKES:

½ cup pecans, chopped

1 (18.25-ounce) box white cake mix, 2 tablespoons reserved for coating the pecans

1 (5-ounce) package instant vanilla pudding mix

½ cup whiskey

½ cup vegetable oil

4 large eggs

FOR THE ICING:

2½ tablespoons all-purpose flour

½ cup whole milk

½ cup granulated sugar

4 ounces (1 stick) unsalted butter, at room temperature

1 teaspoon whiskey

⅔ cup dried cherries, finely chopped

16 walnuts, for garnish

BRING THESE CUPCAKES TO AN OL' FASHIONED BACKYARD barbecue. Whiskey and pecans flavor the moist cupcake, while the dried cherries seem to float in the delicately light icing.

1. Preheat the oven to 350°F. Line a cupcake pan with 16 cupcake liners. Set aside.

2. In a small bowl, coat the pecans with the reserved 2 tablespoons cake mix. Set aside.

3. In a large bowl, combine the pudding mix, cake mix, whiskey, oil, and eggs. Use an electric mixer on medium speed to mix for 3 to 4 minutes, or until smooth. Turn the mixer to low and add the coated pecans.

4. Pour the batter into the prepared cups. Bake for 18 to 22 minutes, or until a toothpick inserted into the center of the cupcake comes out clean. Cool on a wire rack for 5 minutes, or until cool enough to handle. Remove the cupcakes from the pan and cool completely.

5. For the icing, heat the flour and milk in a saucepan until thick, whisking constantly. Set aside to cool.

(continued)

6. In a bowl, use the mixer to beat the sugar and butter until smooth and light in color, and then add the whiskey. Continue mixing as you add the milk mixture. Turn the mixer to medium-high speed and beat until smooth and fluffy. Fold in the cherries. Smooth the icing onto the cooled cupcakes and top each with a walnut.

KATE'S TIP: What's the deal with coating the pecans in cake mix? That simple step will keep the nuts from sinking to the bottom of your cupcakes while baking.

Bourbon Ball Surprise Cupcakes

MY GRANDMOTHER WAS DEFINITELY ONTO SOMETHING WHEN *she created these bourbon balls, which make a wonderful surprise in the center of the cupcakes. Feel free to double the bourbon ball recipe and set them aside as a sweet candy treat!*

1. Begin by making the 12 bourbon balls. In a bowl, combine the wafers, walnuts, cocoa, syrup, and bourbon. Roll the mixture between your hands to make balls, about 1 inch in diameter. Allow them to dry at room temperature, and then roll them in the sugar.

2. Preheat the oven to 350°F. Line a cupcake pan with 12 cupcake liners. Set aside.

3. For the cupcakes, sift together the flour, baking powder, cinnamon, allspice, salt, and nutmeg in a medium bowl. Set aside.

4. In a large bowl, use an electric mixer on medium-high speed to beat together the butter and sugar for 2 minutes, or until well combined. Add the eggs, one at a time, scraping the bowl as needed. Turn the mixer to low speed and alternate between adding the flour mixture and milk in three additions, ending with the flour.

(continued)

Makes 12

FOR THE BOURBON BALLS:

¼ cup vanilla wafers, crushed

¼ cup chopped walnuts

¾ teaspoon cocoa powder

¾ teaspoon light corn syrup

1 tablespoon bourbon

¼ cup confectioners' sugar

FOR THE CUPCAKES:

2 cups cake flour

2 teaspoons baking powder

1½ teaspoons ground cinnamon

½ teaspoon allspice

¼ teaspoon salt

¼ teaspoon ground nutmeg

4 tablespoons unsalted butter, at room temperature

¾ cup dark brown sugar, packed

2 large eggs

¾ cup whole milk

5. Pour the batter into the prepared cups, filling just halfway. Drop the prepared bourbon balls on the batter in each cup. Cover the balls with the remaining batter. Bake for 18 to 22 minutes, or until a toothpick inserted into the side of the cupcake comes out clean. Cool on a wire rack for 5 minutes, or until cool enough to handle. Remove the cupcakes from the pan and cool completely.

6. For the icing, begin by melting the unsweetened chocolate in a double boiler (see page 14), stirring constantly until melted. Set aside.

7. In a bowl, use the mixer on medium speed to beat the butter until creamy. Slowly add the 1 cup sugar, continuing to beat until the mixture becomes light in color. Add the bourbon and melted chocolate, mixing until thoroughly combined. Alternate between adding the milk and the remaining 1 cup sugar, beating until smooth and creamy. Pipe the icing onto the cooled cupcakes.

FOR THE ICING:

2 ounces unsweetened baking chocolate

4 tablespoons unsalted butter, at room temperature

1 cup plus 1 cup confectioners' sugar

1 teaspoon bourbon

¼ cup whole milk

Cosmo Cupcakes

Makes 24

FOR THE CUPCAKES:

1 cup dried cranberries

1 cup vodka

¼ cup orange liqueur

2 cups all-purpose flour

2 teaspoons baking powder

1 teaspoon salt

8 ounces (2 sticks) unsalted butter, at room temperature

2 cups granulated sugar

3 large eggs

Zest from 2 limes, about 2 tablespoons

1 cup sour cream

FOR THE GLAZE:

1½ cups confectioners' sugar, sifted

¼ cup cranberry juice

Zest from 2 limes, about 2 tablespoons

YOU CAN'T GET MUCH GIRLIER THAN A COLD COSMO, OR, better yet ... Cosmo Cupcakes! After you bake these sweet numbers, finish them off with a sexy glaze and a dash of zest. Perfect for a bachelorette party or to start a girl's night out the right way!

1. Preheat the oven to 350°F. Line a cupcake pan with 24 cupcake liners. Set aside.

2. In a food processor, combine the cranberries, vodka, and orange liqueur. Pulse until the cranberries are shredded, but not liquefied. Set aside.

3. In a medium bowl, sift together the flour, baking powder, and salt. Set aside.

4. In a large bowl, use an electric mixer on medium speed to cream together the butter and sugar until light and fluffy. Add the eggs, one at a time. Add the lime zest, sour cream, and the reserved cranberry mixture, blending until well combined. Turn the mixer to low speed and gradually add the flour mixture, blending just until combined.

5. Divide the batter evenly among the cupcake liners and bake for 16 to 20 minutes, or until a toothpick inserted into the center of the cupcake comes out clean. Cool on a wire rack for 5 minutes, or until cool enough to handle. Remove the cupcakes from the pan and cool completely.

6. For the glaze, mix all of the ingredients in a small bowl with a fork until the mixture is smooth. Drizzle the glaze onto the cooled cupcakes.

KATE'S TIP: If the mixture isn't as pink as the Cosmos you're used to, feel free to add two or three drops of red food coloring.

Dark Stout Chocolate Cupcakes

Makes 18

FOR THE CUPCAKES:

1 cup dark stout beer

6 tablespoons salted butter

4 ounces unsweetened baking chocolate

2 cups granulated sugar

¾ cup sour cream

2 large eggs

1 teaspoon vanilla extract

2½ cups all-purpose flour

2 teaspoons baking soda

FOR THE ICING:

1 (8-ounce) package cream cheese, at room temperature

6 ounces white chocolate, melted and cooled

4 ounces (1 stick) salted butter

1 tablespoon dark stout beer

1 cup mini marshmallows, for topping

THESE CUPCAKES ARE RICH AND HANDSOME. THEY'RE PERFECT for St. Patrick's Day parties or any old time you want a comforting bite of yumm. The marshmallows on top look like the frothy head on your favorite dark stout beer.

1. Preheat the oven to 350°F. Line a cupcake pan with 18 cupcake liners. Set aside.

2. Combine the beer, butter, and chocolate in a double boiler (see page 14). Stir the mixture until smooth. When three-quarters of the chocolate has melted, remove the mixture from the heat. Add the sugar, stirring until the granules melt.

3. In a large bowl, combine the sour cream, eggs, and vanilla. Use an electric mixer on medium speed to beat until combined. Slowly add the beer mixture. When smooth, add the flour and baking soda, mixing until smooth.

4. Pour the batter into the prepared cups. Bake for 18 to 22 minutes, or until a toothpick inserted into the center of the cupcake comes out clean. Cool on a wire rack for 5 minutes, or until cool enough to handle. Remove the cupcakes from the pan and cool completely.

(continued)

5. For the icing, beat the cream cheese until fluffy. Slowly add the cooled, melted white chocolate, butter, and beer. Use the mixer on medium-high speed to beat until light and fluffy.

6. Top the cooled cupcakes with the icing and marshmallows.

KATE'S TIP: If you're making these cupcakes for a St. Patrick's Day party, you may want to chop up half a cup of chocolate dinner mints (with the green inside) and mix them in just before distributing the batter into the cupcake liners.

Tequila Sunrise Cupcakes

AH. I THINK WE ALL HAVE A TWISTED STORY OF SOME SORT involving one too many tequilas. These cupcakes not only have that unmistakable taste, but they even look like a good ol' tequila sunrise! They are moist and delicious in every way. Add a bit of fanciness by topping them with paper umbrellas poked through maraschino cherries.

1. Preheat the oven to 350°F. Line a cupcake pan with 12 cupcake liners. Set aside.

2. Use a grater to zest the 2 oranges. Cut them in half and squeeze enough juice to reserve ½ cup. Set aside.

3. In a large bowl, use an electric mixer to beat the egg whites until medium peaks form. Set aside.

4. Beat the butter until smooth. Slowly add the sugar and beat until light and fluffy. Add the egg yolks, one at a time, and then add the orange zest.

5. Sift together the flour, baking powder, baking soda, and salt in a small bowl. In another small bowl, mix together the juice from the 2 oranges and the tequila. Alternate between adding these 2 mixtures to the sugar mixture, while blending on medium speed. Fold the egg whites into the batter.

(continued)

Makes 12

FOR THE CUPCAKES:

2 large oranges

2 large eggs, separated

4 ounces (1 stick) salted butter, at room temperature

¾ cup granulated sugar

1½ cups all-purpose flour

1½ teaspoons baking powder

¼ teaspoon baking soda

¼ teaspoon salt

½ cup tequila

3 to 4 drops red food coloring

3 to 4 drops orange food coloring

FOR THE GLAZE:

1 tablespoon lime juice

1 tablespoon tequila

½ cup confectioners' sugar, sifted

Zest from 1 lime, for garnish

6. Divide the batter into two equal portions. Add several drops of the red food coloring to one of these portions and orange food coloring to the other. Pour the red batter into the bottom of each cupcake liner and top it off with the orange batter.

7. Bake for 16 to 20 minutes, or until a toothpick inserted into the center of the cupcake comes out clean. Cool on a wire rack for 5 minutes, or until cool enough to handle. Remove the cupcakes from the pan.

8. With the cupcakes still warm, poke holes into the top using a toothpick. For the glaze, stir together the lime juice, tequila, and sugar in a small bowl, until smooth. Pour the glaze into the holes in the cupcakes and top with the lime zest.

Jäger® Bomb Cupcakes

Makes 16

FOR THE CUPCAKES:

2 cups all-purpose flour

1¾ teaspoons baking powder

1 teaspoon salt

4 ounces (1 stick) unsalted butter, at room temperature

1 cup granulated sugar

2 large eggs

2 teaspoons vanilla extract

¼ cup Red Bull®

½ cup whole milk

FOR THE GANACHE FILLING:

⅓ cup heavy cream

⅔ cup white chocolate chips

1 tablespoon unsalted butter

1 tablespoon Jägermeister®

FOR THE ICING:

4 ounces (1 stick) plus 2 tablespoons unsalted butter, at room temperature

3 cups confectioners' sugar, sifted

¼ cup Jägermeister®

IT'S GONNA BE A LATE NIGHT. THE SCENT OF RED BULL® WILL have you thinking back to nights of sticky floors, damaged eardrums, and random phone numbers found in your phone. Good thing these cupcakes have a smoother finish!

1. Preheat the oven to 350°F. Line a cupcake pan with 16 cupcake liners. Set aside.

2. In a small bowl, sift together the flour, baking powder, and salt. Set aside.

3. In a large bowl, use an electric mixer on medium speed to cream together the butter and sugar until light and fluffy. Add the eggs, one at a time. Add the vanilla, Red Bull, and milk, mixing until well combined. Turn the mixer to low speed and gradually add the flour mixture, blending just until combined.

4. Divide the batter evenly among the cupcake liners and bake for 16 to 20 minutes, or until a toothpick inserted into the center of the cupcake comes out clean. Cool on a wire rack for 5 minutes, or until cool enough to handle. Remove the cupcakes from the pan and cool completely.

5. Once the cupcakes have cooled completely, use a serrated knife or star-tipped pastry tip to cut a small hole in the top of the cupcakes, about two-thirds of the way to the bottom, big enough for about 1 tablespoon of filling.

6. For the filling, heat the cream over low heat, stirring until simmering. Remove from the heat and pour over the chocolate chips, stirring constantly. Add the butter and Jägermeister, stirring until well mixed. Use a pastry or sandwich bag with a hole in the corner to fill the cupcakes with this mixture.

7. For the icing, use the mixer on medium speed to beat the butter until light and fluffy. Gradually add the sugar, beating until fully combined. Add the Jägermeister and beat until fluffy. Smooth the icing onto the cooled cupcakes.

Rum and Cola Cupcakes

AN OLD FAVORITE, THESE CUPCAKES ARE THE NEXT BEST THING to a night saddled up at your favorite little dive bar. Plus, they're pretty damn cute, just like you! The icing is delicate, fluffy, and marshmallowy, and is extra fancy when piped!

1. Preheat the oven to 350°F. Line a cupcake pan with 24 cupcake liners. Set aside.

2. In a medium bowl, sift together the flour, baking soda, salt, sugar, and cocoa. Set aside.

3. In a large bowl, beat the shortening, buttermilk, cola, and rum. Add the egg and yolks, one at a time. When well mixed, add the flour mixture and beat for an additional 2 minutes, or until smooth.

4. Pour the batter into the prepared cups. Bake for 16 to 20 minutes, or until a toothpick inserted into the center of the cupcake comes out clean. Cool on a wire rack for 5 minutes, or until cool enough to handle. Remove the cupcakes from the pan and cool completely.

5. For the icing, combine all of the ingredients over a double boiler (see page 14) with rapidly boiling water. Use an electric mixer to beat the mixture until it produces stiff peaks. Remove from the heat and continue beating until the mixture becomes thick and shiny. Add a generous dollop of icing to the tops of the cupcakes, or for something extra fancy, use piping bags to decorate them. Serve within one day.

Makes 24

FOR THE CUPCAKES:

2 cups all-purpose flour

1½ teaspoons baking soda

1 teaspoon salt

1⅓ cups granulated sugar

½ cup unsweetened cocoa powder

½ cup butter-flavored shortening, cut into small pieces

⅔ cup buttermilk

½ cup cola

¼ cup rum

1 large egg

2 egg yolks from large eggs

FOR THE ICING:

2 egg whites from large eggs

¾ cup granulated sugar

⅓ cup light corn syrup

⅓ cup cola

1 tablespoon dark rum

¼ teaspoon salt

¼ teaspoon cream of tartar

FAST AND EASY STUFF

⁂

BEING CALLED "FAST AND EASY" CAN SOMETIMES BE A GOOD thing. A really good thing. This section will set the record straight. Put simply, these cupcakes are for the girlie on the go. If you spend your lunch break at your desk, are constantly attached to your phone, or find it hard to have a conversation without thinking of the myriad things you have to do that evening, these recipes were written especially with you in mind. They require fewer ingredients and bowls, and they can be made in less time than it takes for your nails to dry. Plus, they're super-delicious! Bonus!

Fuzzy Navel Cupcakes

Makes 18

FOR THE CUPCAKES:

1 (18-ounce) box orange cake mix

3 large eggs

¾ cup orange juice

½ cup peach schnapps

⅓ cup vegetable oil

½ cup chopped peaches, fresh or canned

FOR THE ICING:

1 (16-ounce) can lemon icing

1 tablespoon peach schnapps

¼ cup chopped peaches, fresh or canned

THESE SWEET BITES ARE QUICK AND EASY WHEN YOU DON'T have much time, but still want a rockin' cupcake. Plus, there's fresh fruit in them, so think of them as one of your five-a-day!

1. Preheat the oven to 350°F. Line a cupcake pan with 18 cupcake liners. Set aside.

2. In a large bowl, combine the cake mix, eggs, orange juice, peach schnapps, and vegetable oil. Use an electric mixer on medium speed to beat the ingredients just until combined. Stir in the chopped peaches by hand. Pour the batter into the prepared cups. Bake for 16 to 18 minutes, or until a toothpick inserted into the center of the cupcake comes out clean. Cool on a wire rack for 5 minutes, or until cool enough to handle. Remove the cupcakes from the pan and cool completely.

3. For the icing, mix the canned icing, peach schnapps, and chopped peaches in a small bowl. Smooth the icing onto the cooled cupcakes.

Mint Grasshopper Cupcakes

THIS IS ANOTHER QUICK AND EASY CUPCAKE FOR GIRLS ON *the go who want to impress. The cupcakes are super rich and will have your guests asking about the secret ingredient: coffee liqueur!*

1. Preheat the oven to 325°F. Line a cupcake pan with 12 cupcake liners. Set aside.

2. In a large bowl, mix the brownie mix, eggs, coffee liqueur, crème de menthe, and vegetable oil. Pour the batter into the prepared cups. Bake for 16 to 18 minutes, or until a toothpick inserted into the center of the cupcake comes out clean. Cool on a wire rack for 5 minutes, or until cool enough to handle. Remove the cupcakes from the pan and cool completely.

3. For the icing, mix the canned icing, crème de menthe, and mini chocolate chips in a small bowl. Dollop the icing onto the cooled cupcakes.

Makes 12

FOR THE CUPCAKES:

1 (18-ounce) box brownie mix

2 large eggs

½ cup coffee liqueur

3 tablespoons crème de menthe

¼ cup vegetable oil

FOR THE ICING:

1 (8-ounce) can cream cheese icing

1½ teaspoons crème de menthe

⅓ cup mini chocolate chips

KATE'S TIP: Want to push these fanciful yet fast and easy cupcakes over the edge? Top off the frosting with a chocolate dinner mint.

Mudslide Cupcakes

Makes 24

FOR THE CUPCAKES:

1 (18-ounce) box chocolate cake mix

1 (3.9-ounce) package chocolate instant pudding mix

2 cups sour cream

4 large eggs

¾ cup vegetable oil

⅓ cup mudslide mix (with alcohol)

¾ cup chocolate chips

FOR THE ICING:

1 (16-ounce) can vanilla icing

2 tablespoons mudslide mix (with alcohol)

Cocoa powder, for dusting

EVERYBODY LIKES TO GET THEIR HANDS DIRTY ONCE IN A WHILE, and these moist and delicious cupcakes provide even the most prim and proper bakers an opportunity to muddy themselves up. But don't worry, you can wash your hands while they bake!

1. Preheat the oven to 350°F. Line a cupcake pan with 24 cupcake liners. Set aside.

2. In a large bowl, mix all of the cupcake ingredients until well combined. Pour the batter into the prepared cups. Bake for 16 to 18 minutes, or until a toothpick inserted into the center of the cupcake comes out clean. Cool on a wire rack for 5 minutes, or until cool enough to handle. Remove the cupcakes from the pan and cool completely.

3. For the icing, use an electric mixer on medium speed to beat the canned icing and mudslide mix until smooth and creamy. Smooth the icing onto the cooled cupcakes and dust with the cocoa.

DIY Cupcake Stencils

So, you probably haven't used or seen stencils since your mom went through that whole "sponge painting stencil borders in every room of the house" phase, but guess what? They can actually be quite useful in baking! Stencils can help add a special something to any cupcake with a naked top or an iced top that's been smoothed flat. You can find tons of stencils at your local craft store or you can use the sexy little stencils included in this cookbook. If you're feeling particularly creative, make your very own designs.

To make your own, you will need:

- a craft knife
- stencil paper (or heavy transparency paper)
- a permanent marker to draw your design
- a board to do the cutting on
- colored sugar crystals, confectioners' sugar, or cocoa powder (sugar crystals work best)

DIRECTIONS:

1. Use a craft knife to cut a 3 × 3-inch square of stencil paper.

2. With a permanent marker, draw whatever design you'd like to see on your cupcakes. Think sexy ladies, flamingoes, letters, hearts, cocktail glasses, stars, etc.

3. Place your stencil paper on top of your cutting board and carefully cut out your design.

4. Hold your stencil directly above your cupcake. Shake the sugar crystals over the stencil or use a sifter to allow the cocoa or confectioners' sugar to evenly fall onto the stencil.

5. Carefully remove your stencil and voilà! You have before you a beautifully decorated cupcake!

DIY Cupcake Wrappers

You can find some adorable and funky cupcake liners all over the Web, but sometimes after you bake, you can't really see all of the details. Cupcake wrappers are made from paper and are wrapped around the liners themselves. You can buy some fancy laser-cut wrappers for oodles of dollars or you can make your own with creative personalization and the template included in this cookbook.

You will need:

- scissors
- this template
- paper from vintage magazines, wallpaper, or wrapping paper (any interesting paper will do!)
- clear tape

DIRECTIONS:

1. Use scissors to cut out this template.

2. Choose a fun selection of paper and trace the template onto your paper. The longer curved edge will be the top edge of the wrapper. You can cut this edge in a curved line or get creative and add zig-zags.

3. Wrap the paper snugly around the cupcake and tape it together.

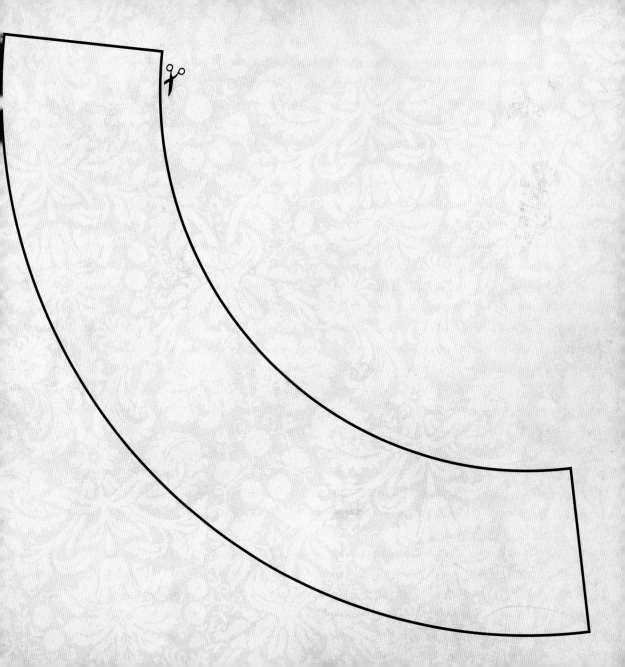

Index

A

Almond liqueur, *in* Grammy Loves
  Pop-Pop Cupcakes, 34–35
Apple Cupcakes, Not Your Granny's, 64

B

Baileys® Irish Cream. *See* Irish cream
  liqueur
Baking tips and equipment, 14–17
Banana liqueur, *in* Banana Upside-Down
  Cupcakes, 21
Banana Upside-Down Cupcakes, 21
Beer
  Belgian Beauty Cupcakes, 73–74
  Car Bomb Cupcakes, 53–55
  Dark and Stormy Cupcakes, 57
  Dark Stout Chocolate Cupcakes,
    102–104
Belgian Beauty Cupcakes, 73–74
Bellini Belle Cupcakes, 75
Bit o' Southern Pride Cupcakes, A,
  94–96
Bloody Mary Cupcakes, 49
Bourbon Ball Surprise Cupcakes, 97–99
Brandy, *in* Not Your Granny's Apple
  Cupcakes, 64
Bright and Cheery Orange Raspberry
  Cupcakes, 50–52
Brownie mix, *in* Mint Grasshopper
  Cupcakes, 117
Butterscotch schnapps, *in* Buttery
  Cinnamony Cupcakes, 22–23
Buttery Cinnamony Cupcakes, 22–23

C

Cake mixes
  Bit o' Southern Pride Cupcakes, A,
    94–96
  Bright and Cheery Orange Raspberry
    Cupcakes, 50–52
  Fuzzy Navel Cupcakes, 114
  Mint Grasshopper Cupcakes, 117
  Mudslide Cupcakes, 118
  Tooty-Fruity Sangria Cupcakes, 63
Car Bomb Cupcakes, 53–55
Carrot Cupcakes, Rum and, 67–68
Champagne
  Bellini Belle Cupcakes, 75
  Champagne Party Cupcakes, 77–78
Cheese, cream. *See* Cream cheese
Cheese, mascarpone, *in* Wine and Cheese
  Party Cupcakes, 89–91
Cherries
  Bit o' Southern Pride Cupcakes, A,
    94–96
  Grammy Loves Pop-Pop Cupcakes,
    34–35
Cherry schnapps, *in* Grammy Loves
  Pop-Pop Cupcakes, 34–35
Chocolate. *See also* White chocolate
  Belgian Beauty Cupcakes, 73–74
  Bourbon Ball Surprise Cupcakes,
    97–99
  Car Bomb Cupcakes, 53–55
  Chocolate Grand Marnier® Cupcakes,
    79
  Cocoa Colada Cupcakes, 24–25
  Dark and Stormy Cupcakes, 57

Dark Stout Chocolate Cupcakes,
  102–104
Grammy Loves Pop-Pop Cupcakes,
  34–35
Mint Grasshopper Cupcakes, 117
Mudslide Cupcakes, 118
Naked Geisha Cupcakes, 83
Oh-So-Decadent Pear and Hazelnut
  Cupcakes, 86–88
Rum and Carrot Cupcakes
  (substitution), 68
Rum and Cola Cupcakes, 111
Top o' the Morning Cupcakes, 42–43
Wine and Cheese Party Cupcakes,
  89–91
Chocolate cake mix, *in* Mudslide
  Cupcakes, 118
Chocolate pudding mix, *in* Mudslide
  Cupcakes, 118
Cinnamon
  Banana Upside-Down Cupcakes, 21
  Bloody Mary Cupcakes, 49
  Bourbon Ball Surprise Cupcakes,
    97–99
  Buttery Cinnamony Cupcakes, 22–23
  Dark and Stormy Cupcakes, 57
  Fancy Pants Golden Gingerbread
    Cupcakes, 81–82
  Fiery Red Velvet Cupcakes, 84
  Naked Geisha Cupcakes, 83
  Not Your Granny's Apple
    Cupcakes, 64
  Oh-So-Decadent Pear and Hazelnut
    Cupcakes, 86–88

Cinnamon *(continued)*
Rum and Carrot Cupcakes, 67–68
Cinnamon schnapps, *in* Fiery Red Velvet
Cupcakes, 84
Cocoa Colada Cupcakes, 24–25
Coconut rum
Cocoa Colada Cupcakes, 24–25
Piña Colada Cupcakes, 27–28
Coffee
Chocolate Grand Marnier® Cupcakes,
79
Grammy Loves Pop-Pop Cupcakes,
34–35
Naked Geisha Cupcakes, 83
Top o' the Morning Cupcakes,
42–43
Coffee liqueur, *in* Mint Grasshopper
Cupcakes, 117
Cosmo Cupcakes, 100–101
Cranberries, *in* Cosmo Cupcakes,
100–101
Cream. *See* Heavy cream
Cream cheese
Buttery Cinnamony Cupcakes, 22–23
Dark and Stormy Cupcakes, 57
Dark Stout Chocolate Cupcakes,
102–104
Fiery Red Velvet Cupcakes, 84
Hot Toddy Cupcakes, 36
Mint Grasshopper Cupcakes, 117
Rum and Carrot Cupcakes, 67–68
White Chocolate and Raspberry
Cupcakes, 44
Cream of tartar
Rum and Cola Cupcakes, 111
Wine and Cheese Party Cupcakes,
89–91

Crème de menthe, *in* Mint Grasshopper
Cupcakes, 117
Cupcake baking tips and tricks, 14–17
Cupcake stencils and wrappers,
120–123

D

Daiquiri, *in* Strawberry Daiquiri Cupcakes,
40–41
Dark and Stormy Cupcakes, 57
Dark chocolate
Belgian Beauty Cupcakes
(substitution), 73–74
Car Bomb Cupcakes, 53–55
Oh-So-Decadent Pear and Hazelnut
Cupcakes, 86–88
Dark Stout Chocolate Cupcakes,
102–104
Designated Driver Cupcakes, 29
DIY cupcake stencils and wrappers,
120–123

E

Eggnog Cupcakes, Spiked, 58–59
"Everything's Gonna Be All White"
Chocolate Cupcakes, 30–32

F

Fancy Pants Golden Gingerbread
Cupcakes, 81–82
Fiery Red Velvet Cupcakes, 84
Framboise beer, *in* Belgian Beauty
Cupcakes, 73–74
Fuzzy Navel Cupcakes, 114

G

Ganache
Car Bomb Cupcakes, 53–55
Jäger® Bomb Cupcakes, 108–109
Oh-So-Decadent Pear and Hazelnut
Cupcakes, 86–88
Ginger beer, *in* Dark and Stormy
Cupcakes, 57
Gingerbread Cupcakes, Fancy Pants
Golden, 81–82
Goldschläger®, *in* Fancy Pants Golden
Gingerbread Cupcakes, 81–82
Grammy Loves Pop-Pop Cupcakes, 34–35
Grand Marnier®. *See* Orange liqueur
Grenadine, *in* Designated Driver
Cupcakes, 29
Guinness®, *in* Car Bomb Cupcakes, 53–55

H

Hazelnut liqueur, *in* Oh-So-Decadent Pear
and Hazelnut Cupcakes, 86–88
Heavy cream
Car Bomb Cupcakes, 53–55
Jäger® Bomb Cupcakes, 108–109
Oh-So-Decadent Pear and Hazelnut
Cupcakes, 86–88
Strawberry Daiquiri Cupcakes, 40-41
Tooty-Fruity Sangria Cupcakes, 63
Honey, *in* Hot Toddy Cupcakes, 36
Hot Toddy Cupcakes, 36

I

Instant pudding mixes. *See* Pudding mixes
Irish cream liqueur
Car Bomb Cupcakes, 53–55

Cocoa Colada Cupcakes, 24–25
Top o' the Morning Cupcakes, 42–43

J

Jägermeister®, *in* Jäger® Bomb Cupcakes, 108–109

L

Limes/lime zest
    Bloody Mary Cupcakes, 49
    Bright and Cheery Orange Raspberry
        Cupcakes (substitution), 52
    Cosmo Cupcakes, 100–101
    Designated Driver Cupcakes, 29
    Mango Margarita Cupcakes, 39
    Minty Mojito Cupcakes, 60–62
    Tequila Sunrise Cupcakes, 105–107
Limoncello Poppy Seed Cupcakes, 33
Long Island iced tea mix, *in* Hot Toddy
    Cupcakes, 36

M

Mango Margarita Cupcakes, 39
Margarita mix, *in* Mango Margarita
    Cupcakes, 39
Marmalade, *in* Tooty-Fruity Sangria
    Cupcakes, 63
Marshmallows, *for* Dark Stout Chocolate
    Cupcakes, 102–104
Mascarpone cheese, *in* Wine and Cheese
    Party Cupcakes, 89–91
Mint Grasshopper Cupcakes, 117
Minty Mojito Cupcakes, 60–62
Mixes, cake. *See* Cake mixes

Mojito Cupcakes, Minty, 60–62
Molasses, *in* Fancy Pants Golden
    Gingerbread Cupcakes, 81–82
Mudslide Cupcakes, 118

N

Naked Geisha Cupcakes, 83
Not Your Granny's Apple Cupcakes, 64
Nutmeg
    Bourbon Ball Surprise Cupcakes, 97–99
    Rum and Carrot Cupcakes, 67–68
    Spiked Eggnog Cupcakes, 58–59
Nuts
    Bit o' Southern Pride Cupcakes, A,
        94–96
    Bourbon Ball Surprise Cupcakes,
        97–99
    Not Your Granny's Apple Cupcakes, 64
    Oh-So-Decadent Pear and Hazelnut
        Cupcakes, 86–88
    Rum and Carrot Cupcakes, 67–68

O

Oh-So-Decadent Pear and Hazelnut
    Cupcakes, 86–88
Orange cake mix, *in* Fuzzy Navel
    Cupcakes, 114
Orange liqueur
    Bright and Cheery Orange Raspberry
        Cupcakes, 50–52
    Chocolate Grand Marnier® Cupcakes,
        79
    Cosmo Cupcakes, 100–101
Orange rum, *in* Rum and Carrot Cupcakes,
    67–68

Oranges/orange zest
    Bright and Cheery Orange Raspberry
        Cupcakes, 50–52
    Chocolate Grand Marnier® Cupcakes,
        79
    Fuzzy Navel Cupcakes, 114
    Hot Toddy Cupcakes, 36
    Tequila Sunrise Cupcakes, 105–107

P

Peach schnapps, *in* Fuzzy Navel Cupcakes,
    114
Peaches
    Bellini Belle Cupcakes, 75
    Fuzzy Navel Cupcakes, 114
Pear and Hazelnut Cupcakes, Oh-So-
    Decadent, 86–88
Pecans
    Bit o' Southern Pride Cupcakes, A,
        94–96
    Not Your Granny's Apple Cupcakes,
        64
Piña Colada Cupcakes, 27–28
Pineapple
    Cocoa Colada Cupcakes, 24–25
    Piña Colada Cupcakes, 27–28
Poppy Seed Cupcakes, Limoncello, 33
Pudding mixes
    Bit o' Southern Pride Cupcakes, A,
        94–96
    Bright and Cheery Orange Raspberry
        Cupcakes, 50–52
    "Everything's Gonna Be All White"
        Chocolate Cupcakes, 30–32
    Mudslide Cupcakes, 118
    Tooty-Fruity Sangria Cupcakes, 63

R

Raisins, *in* Rum and Carrot Cupcakes, 67–68

Raspberries
    Belgian Beauty Cupcakes, 73–74
    Bright and Cheery Orange Raspberry Cupcakes, 50–52
    White Chocolate and Raspberry Cupcakes, 44

Raspberry beer, *in* Belgian Beauty Cupcakes, 73–74

Raspberry liqueur, *in* White Chocolate and Raspberry Cupcakes, 44

Red Bull®, *in* Jäger® Bomb Cupcakes, 108–109

Red Velvet Cupcakes, Fiery, 84

Rum
    Cocoa Colada Cupcakes, 24–25
    Dark and Stormy Cupcakes, 57
    Minty Mojito Cupcakes, 60–62
    Piña Colada Cupcakes, 27–28
    Rum and Carrot Cupcakes, 67–68
    Rum and Cola Cupcakes, 111
    Spiked Eggnog Cupcakes, 58–59
    Strawberry Daiquiri Cupcakes, 40–41

S

Sake, *in* Naked Geisha Cupcakes, 83

Sangria Cupcakes, Tooty-Fruity, 63

Sour cream
    Car Bomb Cupcakes, 53–55
    Cosmo Cupcakes, 100–101
    Dark Stout Chocolate Cupcakes, 102–104
    Minty Mojito Cupcakes, 60–62

Mudslide Cupcakes, 118

Spiked Eggnog Cupcakes, 58–59

Stencils and wrappers, 120–123

Stout
    Car Bomb Cupcakes, 53–55
    Dark Stout Chocolate Cupcakes, 102–104
    Strawberry Daiquiri Cupcakes, 40–41

T

Tequila
    Mango Margarita Cupcakes, 39
    Tequila Sunrise Cupcakes, 105–107

Tooty-Fruity Sangria Cupcakes, 63

Top o' the Morning Cupcakes, 42–43

Triple sec. *See* Orange liqueur

V

Vanilla pudding mix
    Bit o' Southern Pride Cupcakes, A, 94–96
    Bright and Cheery Orange Raspberry Cupcakes, 50–52
    "Everything's Gonna Be All White" Chocolate Cupcakes, 30–32
    Tooty-Fruity Sangria Cupcakes, 63

Vodka
    Bloody Mary Cupcakes, 49
    Cosmo Cupcakes, 100–101

W

Walnuts
    Bit o' Southern Pride Cupcakes, A, 94–96

Bourbon Ball Surprise Cupcakes, 97–99

Rum and Carrot Cupcakes, 67–68

Whiskey
    Bit o' Southern Pride Cupcakes, A, 94–96
    Car Bomb Cupcakes, 53–55

White cake mix, *in* A Bit o' Southern Pride Cupcakes, 94–96

White chocolate
    Dark Stout Chocolate Cupcakes, 102–104
    "Everything's Gonna Be All White" Chocolate Cupcakes, 30–32
    Jäger® Bomb Cupcakes, 108–109
    White Chocolate and Raspberry Cupcakes, 44
    Wine and Cheese Party Cupcakes, 89–91

White chocolate liqueur, *in* "Everything's Gonna Be All White" Chocolate Cupcakes, 30–32

Wine
    Bellini Belle Cupcakes, 75
    Champagne Party Cupcakes, 77–78
    Tooty-Fruity Sangria Cupcakes, 63
    Wine and Cheese Party Cupcakes, 89–91

Wrappers and stencils, 120–123

Y

Yellow cake mix
    Bright and Cheery Orange Raspberry Cupcakes, 50–52
    Tooty-Fruity Sangria Cupcakes, 63

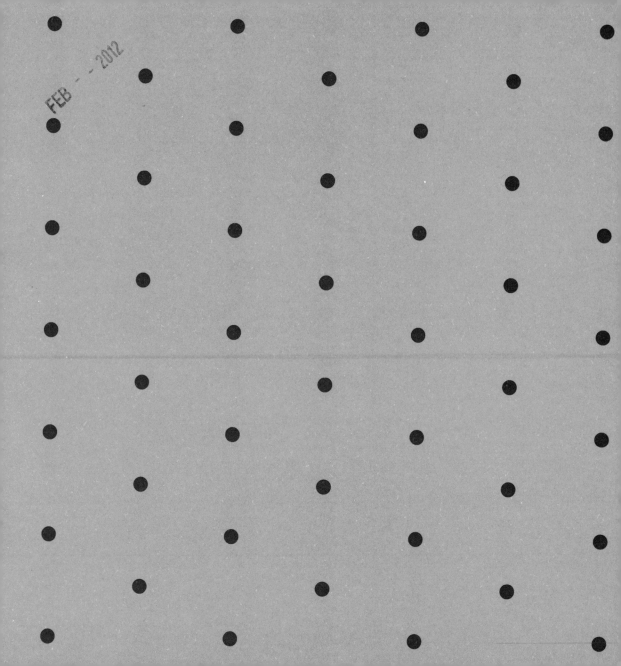